WHEN KINGS SPEAK:
ROYAL SPEECH AND ROYAL PRAYER IN CHRONICLES

SOCIETY
OF BIBLICAL
LITERATURE

DISSERTATION SERIES
J. J. M. Roberts, Old Testament Editor
Charles Talbert, New Testament Editor

Number 93

WHEN KINGS SPEAK:
ROYAL SPEECH AND ROYAL PRAYER IN CHRONICLES

by
Mark A. Throntveit

Mark A. Throntveit

WHEN KINGS SPEAK
Royal Speech and Royal Prayer in Chronicles

Scholars Press
Atlanta, Georgia

WHEN KINGS SPEAK:
Royal Speech and Royal Prayer in Chronicles

Mark A. Throntveit

Ph.D., 1982
Union Theological Seminary

Advisor:
Patrick D. Miller, Jr.

Library of Congress Cataloging-in-Publication Data

Throntveit, Mark A., 1949–
  When kings speak.

  (Dissertation series / Society of Biblical
Literature ; no. 93)
  Originally presented as the author's thesis (Ph.D.)–Union Theological Seminary, 1982.
  Bibliography: p.
  1. Bible. O.T. Chronicles–Criticism, interpreta-
tion, etc. 2. Kings and rulers–Biblical teaching.
I. Title. II. Series: Dissertation series (Society of
Biblical Literature) ; no. 93.
BS1345.2.T48 1987   222'.606   86-15497
ISBN 0-89130-998-5 (alk. paper)
ISBN 0-89130-999-3 (pbk. : alk. paper)

Printed in the United States of America

To the memory of my father,
Thelford Marlin Throntveit

Contents

Acknowledgments

Those readers who are familiar with the Books of Chronicles will recognize my indebtedness to the classic work of E. L. Curtis, A. A. Madsen, Martin Noth, Wilhelm Rudolph and P. R. Ackroyd. Less obvious, though in many ways more influential have been the more recent contributions of R. L. Braun, Sara Japhet and above all, H. G. M. Williamson.

Patrick D. Miller, Jr., my thesis adviser, was a constant source of encouragement throughout the writing of this thesis and serves today as an example of scholarly commitment to the concerns of the church.

Among those who helped me in the preparation of this manuscript, two of my teaching assistants, Paul Barribeau and Kristine Johnson Rufatto, deserve special thanks for their work on the scripture index.

Finally, I would like to express my love for Karol, Trygve and Trevor, whose love and support continue to sustain and refresh me.

M.A.T.

Luther Northwestern Theological Seminary
February 1987

Abbreviations

Abt	Abteilung
AT	Altes Testament
Bd	Band
BDB	Brown-Driver-Briggs, *Hebrew and English Lexicon of the Old Testament*
BH^3	*Biblia Hebraica* (Kittel)
BHS	*Biblia Hebraica Stuttgartensia*
BWANT	Beiträge zur Wissenschaft vom Alten und Neuen Testament
BZAW	Beihefte zur Zeitschrift für die alttestamentliche Wissenschaft
CBQ	*Catholic Biblical Quarterly*
Chr	Chronicles (I and II)
CTM	*Concordia Theological Monthly*
Dan	Daniel
Deut	Deuteronomy
DtrH	The Deuteronomistic History, (Historian)
Eng	English
Esth	Esther
Exod	Exodus
Ezek	Ezekiel
FRLANT	Forschungen zur Religion and Literatur des Alten und Neuen Testaments
FTS	Freiburger theologisches studien
GKC	*Gesenius' Hebrew Grammar*, ed. E. Kautzsch, tr. A. E. Cowley
HAT	Handbuch zum Alten Testament
HSM	Harvard Semitic Monographs
HTR	*Harvard Theological Review*
ICC	International Critical Commentary

Int	*Interpretation*
JBL	*Journal of Biblical Literature*
JNES	*Journal of Near Eastern Studies*
LBH	Late Biblical Hebrew
LXX	Septuagint
LXX^A	Septuagint Alexandrinus
LXX^B	Septuagint Vaticanus
LXX^L	Septuagint Lucianic
MSS	manuscripts
MT	Massoretic Text
NAB	New American Bible
Neh	Nehemiah
OTL	Old Testament Library
RSV	Revised Standard Version
Sam	Samuel (I and II)
SBLMS	*Society of Biblical Literature Monograph Series*
T	Teil
VT	*Vetus Testamentum*
VTSupp	Supplements to Vetus Testamentum
WMANT	Wissenschaftliche Monographien zum Alten und Neuen Testament
ZAW	*Zeitschrift für die alttestamentliche Wissenschaft*
Zech	Zechariah

Unless otherwise noted all translations are those of the author.

1

Introduction

It is certain that the Chronicler has used some form of 2 Samuel and 1, 2 Kings as his primary source. Consequently, in an attempt to discover his unique theological stance, previous scholarship has tended to concentrate upon the parallel or synoptic portions of these works. On the analogy of current criticism in the Synoptic Gospels, by comparing and contrasting the numerous additions, omissions and alterations made to his source, a seemingly consistent picture of chronistic theology emerged. That this picture resulted in a reduction of the Chronicler's value is evidenced in the famous statement of Julius Wellhausen:

> See what Chronicles has made out of David! The founder of the temple and the public worship, the king and hero at the head of his companions in arms has become the singer and master of ceremonies at the head of a swarm of priests and Levites; his clearly cut figure has become a feeble holy picture, seen through a cloud of incense.[1]

Subsequent investigation has done much to clear the air of Wellhausen's "cloud of incense" and enabled us to see more clearly that "feeble holy picture" of David as the Chronicler presents him. Of these scholarly advances, the most important has been the recognition that the Chronicler did not have the MT of Samuel-Kings before him as a source, or *Vorlage,* but rather, a Palestinian text of Samuel-Kings closely related to the LXX, the Hebrew basis of which (at least for Samuel) has been discovered at Qumran.[2] Since Werner Lemke has shown that many of the

---

[1]Julius Wellhausen, *Prolegomena to the History of Ancient Israel* (Cleveland: Meridian Books, 1957), 182.

[2]See Werner E. Lemke, "The Synoptic Problem in the Chronicler's

so-called tendentious theological alterations were already present in the Chronicler's source,[3] it is difficult to deduce his theology solely on the basis of comparing the synoptic portions of the two histories. For this reason, then, this study will concern itself with a significant portion of the non-synoptic material to be found in the books of Chronicles.

A second scholarly advance significant for the understanding of Chronicles has been the growing suspicion that Ezra and Nehemiah are not a part of the Chronicler's work and that they speak to problems in the post-exilic community that were not present at the time of the Chronicler's literary activity. For a century and a half, liberal and conservative Old Testament scholarship alike have accepted the position, first formulated by Leopold Zunz, that the books of Chronicles, Ezra and Nehemiah are a unified whole, which when read sequentially constitute a comprehensive presentation of the history of Israel from Adam to the time of Nehemiah.[4] The four main arguments used to support this position have been conveniently listed by Sara Japhet:

1. The presence of the first verses of Ezra at the end of Chronicles

2. 1 Esdras begins with 2 Chr 35-36 and continues through Ezra

3. The linguistic resemblance between the books as revealed by common vocabulary, syntactic phenomena, and stylistic peculiarities

---

History," *HTR* 58 (1965) 349-63, which summarizes the results of his unpublished Th.D. dissertation, "Synoptic Studies in the Chronicler's History" (Harvard University, 1963); as well as Frank M. Cross, "The Evolution of a Theory of Local Texts," in *Qumran and the History of the Biblical Text,* ed. idem and Shemaryahu Talmon (Cambridge: Harvard University Press, 1975), 306-20 and the bibliography cited there.

[3]Lemke, "Synoptic Problem." For a critique of some of Lemke's other findings see Chapter 4, below.

[4]Leopold Zunz, "Dibre Hajamim oder die Bücher der Chronik," first published in Berlin in 1832, in *Die gottesdienstlichen Vorträge der Juden, historisch entwickelt. Ein Beitrag zur Altertumskunde und biblischen Kritik, zur Literatur- und Religionsgeschichte,* 13-36, zweite, nach dem Handexemplar des Verfassers berichtige und mit einem Register vermahrte Auflage, hrsg. von N. Brüll (Frankfurt a. M.: Verlag von J. Kauffmann, 1892).

4. The alleged uniformity of theological conceptions, expressed both in the material and its selection[5]

In her article, Japhet concentrates upon the last two arguments and convincingly shows that, in the areas of specific technical terms and stylistic peculiarities, the books of Chronicles are so different from Ezra-Nehemiah that "the books could not have been written or compiled by the same author."[6] Less convincing are her arguments concerning the linguistic opposition between the books.[7]

Whereas Japhet concentrated upon the *differences* between the books of Chronicles and Ezra-Nehemiah, H. G. M. Williamson has argued against their common authorship by refuting the alleged linguistic and ideological *similarities* that exist between them as well as countering the first two arguments on Japhet's list.[8]

Against the argument that Chronicles, Ezra, and Nehemiah were originally one book that was divided in the process of canonization and that 2 Chr 36:22-23 = Ezra 1:1-3a was placed on both books as evidence of this process, Williamson argues from internal evidence that there is no precedent for this procedure and, text-critically, the Ezra passage has been added to Chronicles which originally ended at 2 Chr 36:21 (pp. 7-10). The available external evidence shows the books were treated separately in all the canons as far back as we can go (pp. 10-12).

The argument from the present shape of 1 Esdras is shown to be inconclusive since the joining of 2 Chr 35-36 to the Ezra materials was probably made by a translator, i.e. 1 Esdras is not a "fragment" of an original work containing all of Chronicles, and Ezra-Nehemiah material,[9] but both a compilation and a fragment written for a distinct purpose (pp. 12-37).

---

[5]Sara Japhet, "The Supposed Common Authorship of Chronicles and Ezra-Nehemiah Investigated Anew," *VT* 18 (1968) 331-32.

[6]Ibid., 371.

[7]Ibid., 334-41. For a critique of this portion of Japhet's article see Robert Polzin, *Late Biblical Hebrew: Toward an Historical Typology of Biblical Hebrew Prose* (Missoula: Scholars Press, 1976), 54-55; and Mark A. Throntveit, "Linguistic Analysis and the Question of Authorship in Chronicles, Ezra and Nehemiah," *VT* 32 (1982) 201-16.

[8]H. G. M. Williamson, *Israel in the Books of Chronicles* (Cambridge: Cambridge University Press, 1977).

[9]As argued by Karl-Friedrich Pohlmann, *Studien zum dritten Esra. Ein Beitrag zur Frage nach dem ursprünglichen Schluss des chronistischen Geschichtswerkes* (Göttingen: Vandenhoeck und Ruprecht, 1970).

4

Royal Speech and Royal Prayer in Chronicles

Japhet and Williamson have seriously challenged the Zunz hypothesis of the common authorship of these books. A dissenting voice is heard in Robert Polzin who argues for what he calls, "similarity in authorship,"[10] on the grounds of a detailed linguistic analysis. I have shown that linguistic analysis can only display the fact that the author(s) of Chronicles and Ezra-Nehemiah wrote in the linguistic stratum of Late Biblical Hebrew, and that deductions as to individual style and thus, authorship, cannot be made on this basis.[11]

Besides Williamson, who deals with five areas of theological and ideological differences between Chronicles and Ezra-Nehemiah,[12] Roddy L. Braun has written several articles dealing with the ideological antitheses of the two works.[13] It is in this area that the most convincing arguments against common authorship will be found.

David Noel Freedman's programmatic essay dealing with the purpose of the Chronicler is a particularly attractive approach along these lines and has recently drawn a number of advocates. Freedman claims the Chronicler wrote his book to support the messianic hopes the post-exilic community attached to the Davidide Zerubbabel's program of restoration, especially as it centered upon the building of the temple and the reestablishment of the cult, as also seen in the prophecies of Haggai and Zech 1-8.[14] Refinements of this basic interpretation have been offered by Cross and Newsome[15] and Petersen and Porter have expressed their

---

[10]Polzin, 71.

[11]Throntveit, "Linguistic Analysis."

[12]Williamson, *Israel*, 60-68.

[13]See Roddy L. Braun, "The Message of Chronicles: Rally 'Round the Temple," *CTM* 42 (1971): 502-13; idem, "A Reconsideration of the Chronicler's Attitude toward the North," *JBL* 96 (1977) 59-62; idem, "Chronicles, Ezra, and Nehemiah: Theology and Literary History," in *Studies in the Historical Books of the Old Testament*, ed. John A. Emerton (Leiden: E. J. Brill, 1979), 52-64.

[14]David N. Freedman, "The Chronicler's Purpose," *CBQ* 23 (1961) 436-42.

[15]Frank M. Cross, "A Reconstruction of the Judean Restoration," *JBL* 94 (1975) 4-18 = *Int* 29 (1975) 187-201, argues for three editions of the Chronicler's work similar to the two editions of Dtr.:

Chr[1] (ca. 520 B.C.) 1 Chr 10-2 Chr 34 + 1 Esdras 1:1-5:65
Chr[2] (ca. 450 B.C.) 1 Chr 10-2 Chr 34 + *Vorlage* of 1 Esdras
Chr[3] (ca. 400 B.C.) 1 Chr 1-9 + 1 Chr. 10-2 Chr. 36 + the Hebrew recension of Ezra-Nehemiah

Some such structuring seems to be inevitable, however, Williamson's work

general agreement.[16]

Further evidence against the common authorship of these books includes the observation that when Ezra and Nehemiah are investigated apart from the books of Chronicles, as undertaken in the recent commentary of Derek Kidner, no significant change in the interpretation of their theology is produced; this suggests that the theological concerns of Ezra-Nehemiah have prejudiced the interpretation of Chronicles rather than the other way around.[17] Since this study finds itself in agreement with the position of Freedman, Cross and Newsome and thus, denies the common authorship of Chronicles with Ezra-Nehemiah, and also, since a priori, the books of Chronicles may be examined alone as they form a distinct unit within the Canon, comparisons with the books or Ezra and Nehemiah will not be made in the following pages.

A third scholarly advance has to do with the developmental stages of the books of Chronicles and the presence of redaction. There is, however, very little consensus at this point. Following Kittel, earlier scholarship assumed the Chronicler merely collected materials, edited from an earlier Levitical perspective, and combined them with two strands of midrashim into a framework he gleaned from Samuel-Kings.[18] Rothstein-Hänel, in an attempt to account for the presence of Priestly as well as deuteronomistic emphases, postulated two recensions of the Chronicler's original work, one, Priestly, at the time of Nehemiah and a second with deuteronomistic

---

on the traditions of 1 Esdras (Israel, 13-37) makes the addition of that material in Chr[1] and Chr[2] doubtful, and Cross' seeming disinterest in redactional activity upon the editions themselves is surely too simplistic. These criticisms are apparently shared by James D. Newsome, "Toward a New Understanding of the Chronicler and his Purposes," *JBL* 94 (1975) 201-17, who places the Chronicler's work back to 520 B.C. but without the Ezra 1-3 material that Cross, or the Ezra 1-6 material that Freedman attaches.

[16] David L. Petersen, *Late Israelite Prophecy: Studies in Deutero-Prophetic Literature and in Chronicles* (Missoula, Mont.: Scholars Press, 1977); J. R. Porter, "Old Testament Historiography," in *Tradition and Interpretation, Essays by the Members of the Society for Old Testament Study*, ed. G. W. Anderson (Oxford: Clarendon Press, 1979), 152-62.

[17] Derek Kidner, *Ezra and Nehemiah: An Introduction and Commentary* (Downer's Grove: InterVarsity, 1979), cf. my review, *JBL* 100 (1981) 632-3.

[18] Rudolf Kittel, *Die Bücher der Chronik*, Handkommentar zum Alten Testament, Abt. 1, Bd. 6, T. 1 (Göttingen: Vandenhoeck und Ruprecht, 1902).

concerns.[19] Gerhard von Rad has basically agreed with this approach although he notices the Chronicler's greater dependence upon the material in Deuteronomy as well as his frequent divergence from the Priestly tradition.[20] Adam Welch has criticized von Rad at this point for his dependence upon the late dating of the Chronicler's work stemming from von Rad's acceptance of Wellhausen's view that the torah was enacted by Ezra at the time of the Return. Welch suggests that the Chronicler was a Levite who wrote his history to substantiate Levitical claims over against the priests about 515 B.C. and that later the work was liberally annotated by pro-priestly redactors to argue their case.[21]

With the appearance of Noth's work, the tables were turned and what was previously assumed to be later accretion was shown to be the original work of the Chronicler, while those sections emphasizing the Levites, especially the majority of the material in 1 Chr 1-9; 23-27 was seen as later redaction.[22] Wilhelm Rudolph, in basic agreement with Noth, sees many additions to the Chronicler's original work but claims they are not homogeneous.[23] Most recently, Thomas Willi has claimed the majority of these expansions and additions stem from later Levitical concerns.[24]

Whereas Jacob M. Myers treats the material as one piece with only incidental additions and H. G. M. Williamson and Sara Japhet find only slightly more redaction than Myers,[25] this study is most closely aligned with the work of Noth, Rudolph and especially Willi, and sees a substantial amount of Levitical redaction in the books of Chronicles. Since this study is attempting to ascertain the significance of Royal Speeches and Royal

---

[19]J. Rothstein and J. Hänel, *Das Erste Buch der Chronik,* Sellins Kommentar zum Alten Testament, Bd. 18, T. 2 (Leipzig: A. Deichert, 1927).

[20]Gerhard von Rad, *Das Geschichtsbild des chronistischen Werkes* (Stuttgart: W. Kohlhammer, 1930).

[21]Adam Welch, *The Work of the Chronicler, Its Purpose and its Date* (London: Oxford University Press, 1939), 5-6; idem, *Post-Exilic Judaism* (Edinburgh: William Blackwood and Sons, 1935), 242-44.

[22]Martin Noth, *Überlieferungsgeschichtliche Studien I. Die sammelnden und bearbeitenden Geschichtswerke im Alten Testament* (Halle: Max Niemeyer Verlag, 1943).

[23]Wilhelm Rudolph, *Chronikbücher* (Tübingen: J. C. B. Mohr, 1955).

[24]Thomas Willi, *Die Chronik als Auslegung: Untersuchungen zur literarischen Gestaltung der historischen Überlieferung Israels,* (Göttingen: Vandenhoeck und Ruprecht, 1972), especially 194-204.

[25]Jacob M. Myers, *I and II Chronicles,* 2 vols. (Garden City: Doubleday, 1965).

Prayers for the structure and theology of "the Chronicler" and thus, is not explicitly concerned with the transmission of the text, this redactional material will be discussed only when there is some question as to its secondary character, although all the redactional material that appears in the Royal Speeches and Royal Prayers will be indicated by inclusion within square brackets.

In light of the information gained from these advances in the understanding of the books of Chronicles, it seems reasonable, that one way of identifying the Chronicler's unique theological stance, while avoiding the problems inherent in assuming a MT of the Chronicler's source or inclusions of later writings, would be to examine a portion of the non-synoptic passages of Chronicles. That the speeches and prayers ultimately derive from the Chronicler and contain the essence of this thought was recognized at least as early as 1934 when von Rad published his "Die levitische Predigt in den Büchern der Chronik."[26] Martin Noth has established that the speeches and prayers contained in the Former Prophets provide insight into Deuteronomistic theology and structure[27] and Martin Dibelius has provided the same for Luke with the speeches that occur in the book of Acts.[28] Encouraged by these previous studies, this study has chosen to examine the Royal Speeches and Royal Prayers in Chronicles to see if the Chronicler has composed speeches and prayers and placed them on the lips of the kings in such a way that clues to his basic structural framework and theological convictions may be discerned by careful analysis.

While von Rad, Plöger and Rigsby have written on the speeches and prayers of the Chronicler, no one, to my knowledge, has as yet investigated the categories of Royal Speech and Royal Prayer as such.[29]

---

[26] *Festschrift Otto Procksch* (Leipzig, 1934), 113-24 = *Gesammelte Studien zum Alten Testament* (München, 1958), 248-61. For a critique of von Rad's form critical classification see Roddy L. Braun, "The Significance of I Chronicles 22, 28, and 29 for the Structure and Theology of the Work of the Chronicler" (Th.D. dissertation, St. Louis: Concordia Seminary, 1971), 242-49.

[27] Noth.

[28] Martin Dibelius, "The Speeches in Acts and Ancient Historiography," first published in 1949 (1944), in *Studies in the Acts of the Apostles,* ed. Heinrich Greeven (London: SCM Press, 1956), 138-85.

[29] Von Rad, "Levitical Sermon"; Otto Plöger, "Reden und Gebete im deuteronomistischen und chronistischen Geschichtswerk," in *Festschrift für Günther Dehn,* ed. Wilhelm Schneemelcher (Neukirchen: Kreis Moers, 1957), 35-49 = Aus der Spätzeit des Alten Testaments (Göttingen: Vanden-

Newsome has provided an exhaustive analysis of the Chronicler's Prophetic Speech but he limits himself to this category.[30] Thus, the selection
of the Chronicler's Royal Speech and Royal Prayer, as an area to be
examined, would seem to be of significant value.

The intention of the present study, then, is to analyze the Royal
Speeches and Royal Prayers that occur in the books of Chronicles. This
will be the burden of Chapters 2 and 3. After determining which speeches
and prayers constitute these categories, attention will be paid to the
translation, structure and intention of the material. It will be discovered
that the Royal Speeches in Chronicles that are clearly chronistic, i.e. that
are not to be attributed to later redaction, or that have not been simply
transcribed from the Chronicler's source, invariably occur at decisive
points in the narrative. As for the Royal Prayers, it will be seen that they
share formal and structural characteristics with the laments and that they
espouse a favorite doctrine of the Chronicler, namely, the omnipotence of
God and the dependence of his people. These chapters will be exegetical
and descriptive in character and will form the core of the dissertation.

In Chapters 4-7 the results of the research carried out in Chapters 2
and 3 will be applied to four areas of interest in the current discussion
about the Chronicler.

In Chapter 4 the results of our analysis of a significant portion of the
non-synoptic material in Chronicles will be compared with the results
Lemke arrived at by means of his analysis of the synoptic material under
the rubric of the Chronicler's supposed *Tendenz* or theological motivations. It will be shown that three of the specific areas of theological
motivation uncovered by Lemke in the synoptic portions, the Theology of
Theocracy, Pan-Israelism and Retributionism, are present in the non-
synoptic portions as well. On the other hand, two of Lemke's specific
areas of theological motivation, anti-Northern polemic and the Idealization of Pious Kings, are not supported by the non-synoptic material, and
two others, dealing with the Chronicler's supposed concern for matters
pertaining to the Levites and the Cult, are inconclusive. Furthermore, it
will be shown that two other areas of theological motivation may be
detected in the Chronicler's Royal Speeches and Prayers and found in his

---

hoeck und Ruprecht, 1975), 50-66 (references will be made to this edition); Richard O. Rigsby, "The Historiography of Speeches and Prayers in
the Books of Chronicles" (Th.D. dissertation, The Southern Baptist
Theological Seminary, 1973).

[30]James D. Newsome, "The Chronicler's View of Prophecy" (Ph.D.
dissertation, Vanderbilt University, 1973).

alterations of his sources, namely, the concept of "Rest" and the concept of the omnipotence of God and the dependence of his people that is so prominent in the Royal Prayers.

In Chapter 5 the character of 1 Chr 29 will be examined. Since this portion of Chronicles contains both a Royal Speech and a Royal Prayer which recently have been attributed to later redaction, it forms an ideal test case for the applicability of the results obtained in Chapters 2 and 3.

In Chapter 6 the dating and historical setting of the Chronicler will be discussed. New evidence, gained from the examination of the Royal Speeches and Prayers will be presented to argue for a date of ca. 527-515 B.C. and a historical and theological setting of the Chronicler contemporaneous with the prophetic works of Haggai and Zech 1-8.

Finally, in Chapter 7 the significance of the Royal Speeches for understanding the structure of the Chronicler's presentation will be demonstrated by uncovering his periodization of the history of the Monarchy. Not only do the Royal Speeches occur at decisive points in the narrative, but they also give structure and shape to the Chronicler's conceptualization of the monarchy in Judah, which in turn enables us to probe the theological significance of his particular ordering of the material. It will be shown that this structuring is intended to emphasize a conviction that *unity* is the greatest good in the divine economy. This, of course, is at odds with a point of view that interprets Chronicles as anti-Samaritan polemic, such as postulated by Rudolph and others.[31]

---

[31]Rudolph, ix-x; Noth, 164-66, 177-79; both of whom go back to the earlier supposition of Charles C. Torrey, "The Chronicler as Editor and as Independent Narrator," *AJSL* 25 (1909) 200. For arguments to the contrary see Willi, 190-93.

2

Royal Speech in Chronicles

The first task of this chapter will be to determine which speeches constitute the category of Royal Speech and, of those so determined, which speeches are most likely to contain the Chronicler's own distinctive thought. The second task will be to analyze the Chronicler's Royal Speeches in a more detailed manner as to text, translation, and structure. For purposes of comparison, redactional material will be included in brackets, parallel passages between Chronicles and Samuel or Kings will be indicated by the sign (=), and the Chronicles text will be pointed only where it diverges from the *Vorlage*.

I. DETERMINATION OF THE CHRONICLER'S ROYAL SPEECH

The following criteria will be used to determine which speeches in the books of Chronicles belong to the category of the Chronicler's Royal Speech:

1. The speech is on the lips of a king

2. The speech is not part of a conversation or dialogue

3. The speech, though paralleled in the *Vorlage,* has been significantly altered

4. The speech is unique to the Chronicler

Of the instances of direct discourse recorded in Chronicles, sixty-four are spoken by kings, and thus fulfill the requirements of criterion (1). However, many of these speeches are not indicative of the Chronicler's unique theological viewpoint and can be eliminated from consideration on the basis of criteria (2), (3), and (4).

Speeches Occurring in Conversation

A comparison of the occurrences of the verbal root אמר in 2 Samuel, 1, 2 Kings and 1, 2 Chronicles reveals a striking discrepancy in word count. The form ויאמר appears 113 times in Chronicles as compared to 488 times in 2 Samuel-Kings. When the other forms of אמר are tabulated they appear 125 times in Chronicles as compared to 426 times in 2 Samuel-Kings.[1] Examination of the works in question leads to the explanation that while DtrH frequently employs conversations and dialogues to carry the narrative,[2] this practice is rare in the books of Chronicles.[3] For this reason, then, it seems most appropriate to eliminate speeches found in such contexts in Chronicles from consideration on the basis of criterion (2). Twenty-four Royal Speeches fall in this category.[4]

Parallel Speeches with no Tendenz

1. 1 Chr 10:4 = 2 Sam 31:4

	1 Samuel	1 Chronicles
a	וַיֹּאמֶר שָׁאוּל לְנֹשֵׂא כֵלָיו	ויאמר שאול אל-נשא כליו
b	שְׁלֹף-חַרְבְּךָ וְדָקְרֵנִי בָהּ	שלף-חרבך ודקרני בה
c	פֶּן-יָבוֹאוּ הָעֲרֵלִים הָאֵלֶּה	פן-יבואו הערלים האלא
d	וּדְקָרֻנִי	
e	וְהִתְעַלְּלוּ-בִּי	והתעללו-בי

Two alterations of the *Vorlage* appear here. In line (a) the Chronicler

---

[1]Based upon the listings found in S. Mandelkern, *Veteris Testamenti Concordantiae* (Tel-Aviv: Schocken, 1971), 111-29.

[2]E.g., 1 Kgs 13; 18; 19; and 20 where ויאמר is employed, respectively, 10, 17, 10 and 20 times to give structure to the chapters' narratives.

[3]When it does occur, it is usually found in a section that the Chronicler has taken over from his *Vorlage*, as in 1 Chr 21 = 2 Sam 24; 2 Chr 18 = 1 Kgs 22.

[4]1 Chr 11:6 = 2 Sam 5:8; 12:17; 17:1 = 2 Sam 7:1; 21:2, 13, 22, 24 = 2 Sam 24:2, 14, 21, 24; 2 Chr 10:5, 6, 9, 12, 14, 15, 17, 25-26, 29, 33 = 1 Kgs 22:5, 7, 8, 8, 15, 16, 18, 26-27, 30, 34; 35:23.

has employed the preposition אֶל- for לְ. This is a linguistic feature characteristic of the later language. In line (d) the Chronicler has omitted the
repetition of ודקרני "and thrust me through" with reference to the Philistines. No theological *Tendenz* is evident.

2. *1 Chr 11:17, 19 = 2 Sam 23:15, 17*

	2 Samuel	1 Chronicles
a	וַיִּתְאַוֶּה דָוִד וַיֹּאמַר	וַיִּתְאָו דָּוִיד ויאמר
b	מִי יַשְׁקֵנִי מַיִם מִבֹּאר	מי ישקני מים מבּוֹר
	בֵּית-לֶחֶם	בית-לחם
c	אֲשֶׁר בַּשָּׁעַר	אשר בשער
d	וַיֹּאמֶר חָלִילָה לִי יהוה	ויאמר חלילה לי מֵאֱלֹהַי
	מֵעֲשֹׂתִי זֹאת	מֵעֲשׂוֹת זאת
e	הֲדַם הָאֲנָשִׁים הַהֹלְכִים	הדם האנשים הָאֵלֶּה אֶשְׁתֶּה
f	בְּנַפְשֹׁתָם	בְּנַפְשׁוֹתָם
g		כִּי בְנַפְשׁוֹתָם הֱבִיאוּם

In line (a) the Chronicler has used the apocopated form of the Hithpael
imperfect of אוה with no change in meaning and the *plene* spelling of
"David" in accordance with LBH. In line (b) the forms בור/באר frequently
vary and cannot be cited as a tendentious change. In v 19, line (d) the
Chronicler's usual substitution of "God" for "Yahweh" appears as well as
the *plene* spelling of the infinitive construct of עשה and בנפשותם in lines
(f), (g). The "shall I drink" in the Chronicler's line (c), which is lacking in
Samuel is found in the LXX of Samuel (πίομαι) and should be restored to
the MT. Line (g) while lacking in Samuel supplies a reason for David's not
drinking the water which is already contained in the speech and thus is not
tendentious.

3. *1 Chr 13:12 = 2 Sam 6:9*

	2 Samuel	1 Chronicles
a	וַיֹּאמֶר אֵיךְ יָבוֹא אֵלַי	לֵאמֹר הֵיךְ אָבִיא אלי
b	אֲרוֹן יהוה	אֵת ארון הָאֱלֹהִים

Linguistic and orthographic alterations include the spelling of "How" in
line (a) and the substitution of "God" for "Yahweh" as well as the addition
of the sign of the definite object in line (b). The Chronicler's use of the

infinitive construct (לאמר) in line (a) is unusual but hardly has theological implications. The use of the first person in line (a) is possibly tendentious in view of the Chronicler's desire, in this section, to show David bringing the Ark to Jerusalem. However, this differs only slightly from the Samuel reading.

4. 1 Chr 14:11 = 2 Sam 5:20

	2 Samuel	1 Chronicles
a	וַיֹּאמֶר פָּרַץ יהוה אֶת-אֹיְבַי	ויאמר דָּוִיד פרץ הָאֱלֹהִים את-אוֹיְבַי
b	לְפָנַי כְּפֶרֶץ מָיִם	בְּיָדִי כפרץ מים

In line (a) only linguistic and orthographic changes occur: the substitution of "God" for "Yahweh" and the *plene* spelling of "my enemies." The instrumental "by my hand" instead of "before me" in line (b) is possibly tendentious, but since "God/Yahweh" is the subject in both cases, the difference in meaning is too slight to be considered theologically motivated.

5. 1 Chr 19:2, 5 = 2 Sam 10:2, 5

	2 Samuel	1 Chronicles
a	וַיֹּאמֶר דָּוִד אֶעֱשֶׂה-חֶסֶד	ויאמר דָּוִיד אעשׂה-חסד
b	עִם-חָנוּן בֶּן-נָחָשׁ	עם-חנון בן-נחשׁ
c	כַּאֲשֶׁר עָשָׂה אָבִיו עִמָּדִי חֶסֶד	כִּי-עשׂה אביו עִמִּי חסד
d	וַיֹּאמֶר הַמֶּלֶךְ שְׁבוּ בִירֵחוֹ	ויאמר המלך שבו בירחו
e	עַד-יְצַמַּח זְקַנְכֶם וְשַׁבְתֶּם	עד אֲשֶׁר-יצמח זקנכם ושבתם

The accounts are almost identical, only the *plene* spelling of "David" in line (a) and the linguistic change עמדי/עמי in line (c) differ. If the אשר of line (c) was written in its shortened form (שׁ) the כי is easily accounted for. In any case, the theological meaning of the two speeches is identical.

6. 2 Chr 6:1, 2, 4-11 = 1 Kgs 8:12, 13, 15-21

Due to the length of this speech it will not be reproduced in parallel columns. Besides the usual linguistic and orthographic alterations we have noticed earlier, the major changes to the *Vorlage* are the Chronicler's apparent addition of vv 5b-6a, "and I chose no man as prince over my people Israel; but I have chosen Jerusalem that my name may be there . . ." and his omission of the reference to the Exodus in 1 Kgs 8:21bβ, "when he brought them out of the land of Egypt." Most commentators recognize that the Chronicler's apparent addition of vv 5b-6a was originally in the Kings account as well. It has fallen out of the text due to homoioteleuton of להיות שמי שם as suggested by the LXX[B].[5] On the other hand, the omission of the reference to the Exodus is surely tendentious and occurs elsewhere in the work.[6] However, it is inappropriate to make too much of this omission as the Exodus is clearly referred to in v 5.[7]

7. 2 Chr 16:3 = 1 Kgs 15:19

	1 Kings	2 Chronicles
a	בְּרִית בֵּנִי וּבֵנֶךָ	ברית בני ובנך
b	בֵּין אָבִי וּבֵין אָבִיךָ	וּבֵין אבי ובין אביך
c	הִנֵּה שָׁלַחְתִּי לָךְ	הנה שלחתי לך
d	שֹׁחַד כֶּסֶף וְזָהָב	כסף וזהב
e	לֵךְ הָפֵרָה אֶת-בְּרִיתְךָ	לך הָפֵר בריתך
f	אֶת-בַּעְשָׁא מֶלֶךְ-יִשְׂרָאֵל	את-בעשא מלך-ישראל
g	וְיַעֲלֶה מֵעָלָי	ויעלה מעלי

The accounts are almost identical. The "and" of line (b) has strong support from Hebrew MSS and the versions in the Kings text, and the omission of "gift" in line (d) is attested in the LXX. The variant form of the imperative of פרר in line (e) does not alter the sense.

8. 2 Chr 24:5-6 = 2 Kgs 12:4, 5, 7

Gray's observation that the Kings text may have suffered corruption

---

[5]See John Gray, *I & II Kings*, revised ed.; OTL (Philadelphia: Westminster, 1964), 214.

[6]For possible explanations see Robert North, "Theology of the Chronicler," *JBL* 82 (1963) 369-81; Williamson, *Israel*, 64-65; and especially Peter R. Ackroyd, "History and Theology in the Writings of the Chronicler," *CTM* 38 (1967) 510-12.

[7]Cf. Lemke, "Synoptic Studies," 38-39, who sees no *Tendenz* here, only a case of "too much from too little." The Chronicler has simply abridged the text.

from Exod 30:12f., a later text, seems to be preferable over the maze of textual emendations usually suggested for this passage.[8] Without a fairly certain text in Kings, comparison with the Chronicler is hazardous, especially since the Chronicler's text reflects the Exodus passage (Exod 30:16). Theologically, money is being collected to repair the temple in both passages.

9. 2 Chr 25:18-19 = 2 Kgs 14:9-10

	2 Kings	2 Chronicles
a	הַחֹוחַ אֲשֶׁר בַּלְּבָנֹון	
b	שָׁלַח אֶל-הָאֶרֶז אֲשֶׁר בַּלְּבָנֹון	
c	לֵאמֹר תְּנָה-אֶת-בִּתְּךָ לִבְנִי לְאִשָּׁה	
d	וַתַּעֲבֹר חַיַּת הַשָּׂדֶה אֲשֶׁר בַּלְּבָנֹון	identical
e	וַתִּרְמֹס אֶת-הַחֹוחַ	
f		אָמַרְתָּ
g	הַכֵּה הִכִּיתָ אֶת-אֱדֹום	הִנֵּה הכית את-אדום
	וּנְשָׂאֲךָ לִבֶּךָ	ונשאך לבך
h	הִכָּבֵד וְשֵׁב בְּבֵיתֶךָ	לְהַכְבִּיד עַתָּה שָׁבָה בביתך
i	וְלָמָּה תִתְגָּרֶה בְּרָעָה	לָמָה תתגוה ברעה
	וְנָפַלְתָּה	וְנָפַלְתָּ
j	אַתָּה וִיהוּדָה עִמָּךְ	אתה ויהודה עמך

Both passages display textual problems. In Kings, Gray suggests reading לְהִכָּבֵד "to glorify yourself" at the beginning of line (h), arguing that it has fallen out due to haplography.[9] Curtis likewise suggests that לְהִכָּבֵד was the original reading of line (h), as witnessed in the Vulgate,[10] and which draws the texts closer together. "You have said," in line (f) is probably a chronistic insertion which precipitated the textual problems. Once again, however, the theological message of the two passages is too close to accuse the Chronicles passage of theological motivation.

The above speeches display no apparent tendentious alterations of the

---

[8]Gray, *Kings,* 584.

[9]Ibid., 606.

[10]E. L. Curtis and A. A. Madsen, *A Critical and Exegetical Commentary on the Books of Chronicles* (New York: Charles Scribner's Sons, 1910), 446.

Vorlage and, on the basis of criterion (3), may safely be eliminated from consideration for determining the Chronicler's theology.

Parallel Speeches Displaying <u>Tendenz</u>

One reference in 1 Chronicles and two references in 2 Chronicles, though paralleled, display tendentious changes.

1. 1 Chron 17:1 = 2 Sam 7:1, 2

	2 Samuel	1 Chronicles
a	וַיְהִי כִּי-יָשַׁב הַמֶּלֶךְ בְּבֵיתוֹ	ויהי כַּאֲשֶׁר ישב דָּוִיד בביתו
b	וַיהוה הֵנִיחַ-לוֹ מִסָּבִיב	
c	מִכָּל-אֹיְבָיו:	
d	וַיֹּאמֶר הַמֶּלֶךְ אֶל-נָתָן הַנָּבִיא	ויאמר דָּוִיד אל- נתן הנביא
e	רְאֵה נָא אָנֹכִי יוֹשֵׁב בְּבֵית אֲרָזִים	הִנֵּה אנכי יושב בבית הָאֲרָזִים
f	וַאֲרוֹן הָאֱלֹהִים יֹשֵׁב בְּתוֹךְ הַיְרִיעָה	וארון בְּרִית-יְהֹוָה תַּחַת וְרִיוֹת

While the actual speeches display only minor changes such as "David" for "the King" (lines a and d), "behold!" for "see, now" and "The house of cedars" for "a house of cedars" (line e), and "the ark of the covenant of Yahweh" for "the ark of God," and "under curtains" for "in the midst of the curtain" (line f), and are couched in a dialogue, the framework of the speech in Chronicles has an important omission in lines (b), (c) "now Yahweh had given him rest from all his enemies." It will be seen later that the Chronicler scrupulously avoids attributing "rest" to David.

2. 2 Chr 2:2-9 (Eng 2:3-10) = 1 Kgs 5:17-23 (Eng 5:3-9)

Again, due to the length of the passages, they will not be reproduced. The occasion of both these speeches is the same, a letter to Huram/Hiram from Solomon. The following elements of 1 Kings have been omitted by the Chronicler:[11]

---

[11]Ibid., 320-21.

1. The embassy from Hiram to Solomon (1 Kgs 5:15): This omission emphasizes Solomon's initiating the Temple-building process. In 1 Kings it is Hiram who wishes to continue the relationship with David.

2. David's hindrance in building the temple due to his being occupied with the wars (1 Kgs 5:17): For the Chronicler it was not a question of being too busy with warfare that hindered David's building of the temple, but rather that his "bloody hands" made him an inappropriate builder (1 Chr 22:8).

3. The rest given to Solomon (1 Kgs 5:18): This is probably due to the fact that this important theme for the Chronicler was dealt with in the Davidic speeches of 1 Chronicles.

4. The promise of Yahweh to David (1 Kgs 5:19): Again, a prominent theme in 1 Chr 22:8-19.

Elements added by the Chronicler generally deal with elaborating the purpose to be served by the temple:

1. Huram's dealings with David (2 Chr 2:2), to reinforce the ties between David and Solomon and further depict the reigns as a unity.

2. A description of the temple as a place of worship and as being very large (2 Chr 2:3-5).

3. Rhetorical questions emphasizing the chronistic theme of his people (2 Chr 2:5).

4. The actual intent of the letter, as shown by the introductory ועתה, is a request for an engraver skilled in metal and cloth as well as special woods (2 Chr 2:6-8a) to provide magnificence for the temple, as the Chronicler says in v 8b: "for the house I am to build will be great and wonderful."

These alterations show that the Chronicler has considerably changed the intent of Solomon's letter and justifies its retention as a chronistic Royal Speech.

3. 2 Chr 34:21 = 2 Kgs 22:13

	2 Kings	2 Chronicles
a	לְכוּ דִרְשׁוּ אֶת-יהוה בַּעֲדִי	לכו דרשו את-יהוה בעדי
b	וּבְעַד-הָעָם וּבְעַד כָּל-יְהוּדָה	ובעד הנשאר בישראל וביהודה
c	עַל דִּבְרֵי הַסֵּפֶר הַנִּמְצָא הַזֶּה	על דברי הספר אשר נמצא
d	כִּי-גְדוֹלָה חֲמַת יהוה אֲשֶׁר-הִיא נִצְּתָה בָנוּ	כי-גדולה חמת יהוה אשר נתכה בנו
e	עַל אֲשֶׁר לֹא שָׁמְעוּ אֲבֹתֵינוּ עַל-דִּבְרֵי הַסֵּפֶר הַזֶּה	על אשר לא-שמרו אבותינו את-דבר יהוה
f	לַעֲשׂוֹת כְּכָל-הַכָּתוּב עָלֵינוּ	לעשות ככל-הכתוב על-הספר הזה

Minor variations not indicative of *Tendenz* include the rendering "*the* book that is found" for "*this* book that is found" (line c), Yahweh's wrath being "poured out upon" the people rather than "kindled against" them (line d), because their fathers "did not keep the word of Yahweh" instead of "did not obey the words of this book" (line c), and to do this according to "this book" instead of "concerning us." This last variation is perhaps explained by two MSS of Kings reading עליו "concerning *it*," a reading attested to in the LXX[L] as εν αυτω which is closer to the Chronicler's text. However, there is one variation that is clearly tendentious in line (b). 2 Kings reads: "Go, inquire of Yahweh for me, and for the people, and for all Judah. . . ." The Chronicler, to show his concern for the re-unification of the people, alters this to read: "Go, inquire of Yahweh for me, and for those who are left in Israel and in Judah . . ."

These three texts, then, though paralleled by their *Vorlagen,* must be seen as chronistic on the basis of criterion (3).

Royal Speeches in Chronicles

Twenty-six speeches in the books of Chronicles fulfill the criteria established at the beginning of the chapter.[12] These speeches will now be analyzed as to text, translation and redaction.

---

[12] 1 Chr 13:2-3; 15:2, 12-13; 17:1; 22:1, 5, 7-16, 18-19; 23:25-32; 28:2-10, 20-21; 29:1-5, 20; 2 Chr 2:3-10; 8:11; 13:4-12; 14:7; 19:6-7, 9-11; 20:20; 28:23; 29:5-11, 31; 30:6-9; 32:7-8; 34:21; 35:3-6.

II. ANALYSIS OF ROYAL SPEECH

In this section the Royal Speeches will be grouped according to their structure. This structural grouping will not be concerned to find *Gattungen* that may or may not occur in the Ancient Near East or even in the Old Testament, but seeks to organize the speeches made by kings in Chronicles into categories with shared structural characteristics.

In an appendix to his dissertation, Roddy L. Braun has attempted an initial classification of the speech forms found in Chronicles.[13] Since all the speeches, except brief responses by the people, are delivered by kings, prophets or priests/Levites, Braun examines these three categories of speech with the addition of prayers.[14] With regard to Royal Speech, Braun discovers three groups on the basis of form and content:

1. Rationales for certain actions: 1 Chr 22:5; 2 Chr 8:11

2. Edicts: 1 Chr 15:2, 12f.; 22:1; 2 Chr 24:5-6; 25:16; 29:31; 35:36 [*sic*]

3. Orations: 1 Chr 2:2-9; 13:4-9 [*sic*]; 14:6; 19:6, 7, 9-11; 20:20; 29:4-11, 31; 30:6-9; 32:6-8[15]

Braun observes that the use of imperatives or their equivalents to introduce the major concern of the speech is the most noteworthy characteristic of the edicts and orations, with the edicts usually consisting of a single clause. An historical retrospect, referring to the distant past or the immediate situation frequently appears in the orations and further differentiates this group.[16]

Besides these formal characteristics, Braun notes a similarity in the content of the Royal Speeches in that they are usually concerned with cultic places and objects, especially the temple. Royal Speeches to the troops before war (2 Chr 13:4-12; 20:20; 32:6-8; 14:7) occur frequently as well, and only Jehoshaphat's speech to the judges (2 Chr 19:6, 7, 9-11) does not fit in these two categories.[17]

---

[13]Braun, "Significance," 225-49.
[14]Ibid., 227.
[15]Ibid., 228.
[16]Ibid., 229.
[17]Ibid., 230-31.

This dissertation is now in a position to extend Braun's preliminary classifications with regard to Royal Speech by gaining more precision into what constitutes each of these groups. Descriptive formal characteristics will be presented for each and a discussion of each speech's classification will be included. It will also be shown that, contrary to Noth, the speeches do regularly occur at turning points in the narrative and thus provide a structural framework for the Chronicler's work.

Edicts

The descriptive formal characteristics of this group are as follows:

1. A specific audience is addressed

2. An imperative or its equivalent is used to introduce the main point of the speech

3. The action called for by the imperative is immediately described in the narrative as carried out by the audience

Five of the Royal Speeches belong to this group[18] and will be discussed in the order of their appearance in Chronicles.

1. 1 Chr 15:11a [11b], 12-15

11. Then David called for Zadok and Abiathar the priests, [and for the Levites, for Uriel, Assiah, Joel, Shemaiah, Eliel and Aminadab],[19] 12. and said to them:
    > You are the heads of the fathers' houses of the Levites; sanctify yourselves, you and your brothers, so that you may bring up the ark of the Lord, the God of Israel, to the tent[20] which I have prepared for it. 13. For why[21]

---

[18]1 Chr 15:12-13; 22:5; 29:20; 2 Chr 29:31; 35:3-6.

[19]See Willi, 196, for the redactional character of this addition of the Levites.

[20]For the reading -ה האהל "the tent which" that has fallen out of the text, see Rudolph, 116.

[21]למבראשונה is not a word. To make sense of the passage it is necessary to read לָמֶּה בראשונה "for why, at first," delete לא אתם and supply the athnach after בנו making verse 13a a question and 13b its answer. Cf.

did the Lord our God make an outburst against us at
first? Because we did not seek him according to the
ordinance.

14. So the priests and the Levites sanctified themselves to
bring up the ark of the Lord, the God of Israel. 15. And the
Levites carried the ark of God upon their shoulders with
the poles, as Moses had commanded according to the word
of the Lord.

That this speech is an edict is shown by the particular audience
addressed, Zadok and Abiathar, the priests (v 11), the use of the imperative התקדשו "sanctify yourselves" (v 12) which introduces the primary
concern of the speech and the narrative of vv 14-15 which immediately
reports the action taken, in response to the imperative, by the audience
addressed.

The speech thus occurs at a turning point in the narrative. The goal of
chaps. 13-16 is the bringing of the ark. Here, in this speech David's commissioning of the proper bearers of the ark insures its safe transport by
following the prescriptions of the Law. Thus, the disaster of Uzza in chap.
13 is avoided.

2. 1 Chr 22:5

Then David said (to himself):[22]

Solomon my son is young and inexperienced, but the
house to be built for Yahweh must be exceedingly
magnificent, famous and glorious throughout all lands;
therefore, I will make preparation for it.

So David provided materials in great quantity before his
death.

Braun has classified this speech as a rationale.[23] His case could be
argued on the basis of translating the initial ו of ויאמר as "For" as does

---

BDB, 912; and Arnold B. Ehrlich, *Randglossen zur hebräischen Bibel, textkritisches, sprachliches und sachliches*, Siebenter Band (Leipzig: J. C.
Hinrich, 1914), 340.

[22]BDB, 56 lists as the second meaning of אמר "say in the heart,"
"think." Kittel, 83, renders, "David dachte dabei." Curtis explains, "'For
David said to himself' is better than 'and David said, etc.,' since v. 5a
states the reason for David's preparation as narrated in vv. 2-4," (256).

[23]Braun, "Significance," 228.

RSV. However, Ackroyd has recognized this speech as introducing "the commissioning of Solomon and is therefore better opened without RSV's 'For.'"[24] Also, the characteristics of the rationale, as will be presented in this dissertation, are not present while those of the edict are. David is addressing himself, the cohortative אכינה is employed to introduce the main point of the speech and the concluding clause immediately reports the action taken in response to the imperative by the audience addressed.

As Braun's dissertation has convincingly shown, 1 Chr 22, 28 and 29 form a transition unit in the Chronicler's work linking the reigns of David and Solomon. Thus, this introductory speech to the commissioning of Solomon may be said to occur at a decisive turning point in the narrative.

3. 1 Chr 29:20

> Then David said to all the assembly:
>   Now bless the Lord your God.
> And all the assembly blessed the Lord, the God of their
> fathers, and bowed their heads, and worshipped the Lord,
> and did obeisance to the king.

Braun does not categorize this speech, either. Once again all the characteristics of the edict are present. A definite audience is addressed, the imperative ברכו-נא is used to introduce the burden of the speech and the narrative immediately reports the audience responding with the action called for by the imperative.

The speech, in calling for the blessing of God by the people, indirectly serves as an appeal for the acceptance of Solomon in that 1 Chr 22, 28, 29 have portrayed Solomon as God's chosen king.[25] Thus, the speech, which inaugurates the celebration of Solomon's coronation, is most definitely a turning point in the narrative.

---

[24]Peter R. Ackroyd, *I & II Chronicles, Ezra, Nehemiah: Introduction and Commentary* (London: SCM Press, 1973), 78.

[25]1 Chr 28:6, 10. See Roddy L. Braun, "Solomon, the Chosen Temple Builder: The Significance of 1 Chronicles 22, 28, and 29 for the Theology of Chronicles," *JBL* 95 (1976) 588-90.

4. 2 Chr 29:[31]

[Then Hezekiah answered the people[26] and said:
   Now, offer richly to the Lord,[27] draw near and bring
   sacrifices for[28] thank offerings to the house of the
   Lord.
So, the assembly brought sacrifices for thank offerings and
generous[29] burnt offerings.]

Braun shows some confusion here as he lists this speech as both an
edict and an oration.[30] That it is an edict is clear from the presence of a
specific audience ("the people" if one accepts this addition to the text, or
"the assembly" if one does not), an imperative אתם מלאו introducing the
intent of the speech, and the assembly's response to the imperative.

However, the attribution of the speech to the Chronicler is question-
able. The response itself is suspicious in that there is nothing previous in
the narrative for Hezekiah to respond to, especially if Willi is correct in
regarding vv 25-30 as a secondary expansion.[31] Secondly, the problematic
expression יד מלא is paralleled in 1 Chr 29:5 in the non-technical sense. It
will be shown on other grounds that 1 Chr 29:5 is from a later hand.[32] The
appearance of the root נדב is also closely associated with the secondary
passages of 1 Chronicles 29. Conceivably, the same redactor who was
responsible for 1 Chr 29:1-9 was responsible for this addition as well.

---

[26]See Rudolph, 298 and the following note.

[27]Since יד מלא is a technical term for the dedication of priests, the
speech appears to be addressed to them. However, the preceding report
described no dedication of priests and, as Ehrlich claims (376) one cannot
dedicate oneself in the Old Testament, but must be dedicated by another.
Also, it is clear from v 31b that it is the assembly (הקהל) which is being
addressed. Thus, we should add לעם before ויאמר, the עם having dropped
out due to the confusion of the ע in ויער, and the ל at a later date
because it was now irrelevant (Rudolph, 298) and read אתם מלאו "you fill"
for מלאתם with Ehrlich (376) and compare the similar construction in 1 Chr
29:5. Literally, the text would read, "You give to Yahweh with full hands."

[28]The ו is epexegetic, see Myers, *II Chronicles*, 169.

[29]The usual translation, "and all who were of a willing heart brought
burnt offerings," (RSV, which supplies "brought") fails to see that the
וכל-נדיב לב is bound to the עולות and so means "generous, liberal" with
Ehrlich, 376.

[30]Braun, "Significance," 228.

[31]Willi, 200.

[32]See Chapter 5.

5. 2 Chr 35:3aα[3bβ-4],5-6

3. And he said [to the Levites who taught[33] all Israel and who
were holy to the Lord:
> Put the holy ark in the house which Solomon the son of
> David, king of Israel, built; it will be a burden upon your
> shoulders no longer. (Now serve) the Lord your God and
> his people Israel. 4. Prepare yourselves according to
> your fathers' houses by your divisions, according to the
> writing of David, king of Israel, and according to the
> writing of Solomon his son.] 5. Stand in the holy place
> according to the groupings of the fathers' houses of your
> brothers the lay people (so that for each father's house
> of the lay people there is a part of a father's house of
> the Levites).[34] 6. Now, slaughter and skin[35] the pass-
> over animals and prepare for your brothers, to do
> according to the word of the Lord by Moses.

Elimination of the redactional material reveals this speech to be the
Chronicler's final edict. It is addressed to the priests, whom Josiah has
just appointed to their offices, and seeks to encourage them (v 2). This
main point of the speech is introduced by the imperatives, "stand,"
"slaughter" and "skin" (vv 5f.) and with the removal of the secondary
material,[36] the priests' response to the action called for in the imperatives is immediately reported in the narrative of vv 10b-11: "So, the
priests slaughtered the passover animals and sprinkled the blood[37] from
their hand, and [the Levites][38] skinned them."

It has been shown that the edicts are all directed to a specific audience, contain an imperative or its equivalent to introduce the major

---

[33]Reading the Qere with many MSS, המבינים. The Kethib, המבונים is a
substantive.

[34]The Hebrew is obscure. The translation reflects Rudolph's proposal
that ולכל-בית-אב לבני העם ה- has fallen out of the text due to homoio-
eleuton (328).

[35]והתקדשו "and sanctify yourselves" cannot be correct as it would have
to precede the slaughtering of the lambs. Thus, והפשיטו "and skin" must
be the correct reading here, as in v 11, see Ehrlich, 384.

[36]For vv 8b-10a see Willi, 201. That vv 7-8a are also redactional is
clear from their similarity to 1 Chr 29:2-9; 2 Chr 30:24.

[37]הדם has fallen out by homoioteleuton as shown by its appearance in
the LXX and Vulgate.

[38]On the redactional character of "the Levites" see Willi, 201.

concern of the speech and the action called for is immediately described in the narrative as being carried out by those addressed.

Rationales

The descriptive formal characteristics of this group are as follows:

1. In contrast with the edicts and orations, no specific audience is addressed.

2. In contrast with the edicts and orations, no imperatives or their equivalents are used to introduce the burden of the speech.

3. In contrast with the edicts and orations, no action in response to the speech is described in the following narrative.

4. The speech provides some rationale for a cultic action.

Five Royal Speeches may be so classified[39] and will be dealt with according to their appearance in Chronicles.

1. 1 Chr 15:[2]

[Then David said:
   No one is to carry the ark of God but the Levites, for the Lord chose them to carry the ark of the Lord[40] and to minister to him forever.]

This chapter has suffered a great deal of later redaction due to the opportunity presented the redactor of supplementing the account with references to the Levites. Willi and Rudolph are agreed that vv 4-10, 11b,

---

[39]1 Chr 5:2; 22:1; 2 Chr 8:11; 23:25-32; 28:23.

[40]Many MSS read האלהים at this point. The originality of יהוה can be maintained, however, by comparison with the LXX which lacks the phrase "to carry the ark of Yahweh." Since the word immediately before the lacuna is κυριος (יהוה) and the last word of the lacuna must be either יהוה or האלהים, the suggestion that the phrase originally ended with יהוה and dropped out by homoioteleuton immediately presents itself.

16-24 are from a later hand, and Willi thinks vv 27aβ and 28aβ are also to be attributed to him.[41]

In light of the composite nature of this chapter, David's speech looks suspiciously like an insertion. The speech seems out of place, breaking the natural flow of the narrative between vv 1 and 3 which describe David's preparations for the ark and his assembling of all Israel to bring the ark up into Jerusalem. The speech would be more appropriate *after* David had assembled the people. A comparison of the ways the Chronicler introduces his Royal Speeches shows this speech to be somewhat irregular also. No other Royal Speech introduction begins with אז אמר דויד. In fact, the only Royal Speeches that approximate this form (1 Chr 23:25, כי אמר דויד and 2 Chr 8:11, כי אמר), in that they use a particle followed by a Qal perfect, will be shown to be redactional on other grounds. Thus, 1 Chr 15:2 appears to be a later addition.

If this judgment on the redactional character of 1 Chr 15:2 is incorrect, and the speech does, in fact, come from the Chronicler, then it must be classified as a rationale and not as an edict as Braun has classified the speech and as Ackroyd seems to agree by calling it a "declaration, almost a decree."[42] But there are no imperatives and no specific audience mentioned, neither is there a report of any action resulting from the speech that would allow Braun's classification. Furthermore, Ackroyd goes on to state: "This is a reiteration of the injunction found in Deut 18:8, so that it may be clear that action is to be in accordance with the law."[43] This would seem to indicate that the speech is delivered to provide a rationale for the cultic action of bearing the ark. Thus, despite its redactional character in the books of Chronicles, 1 Chr 15:2 must be considered to be a rationale.

2. 1 Chr 22:1

Then David said:
This is the house of the Lord God, and this is the altar of burnt offering for Israel.

Braun regards this brief speech as an edict.[44] But, once again, there are no imperatives. Furthermore, Braun may have missed the relationship

---

[41]Rudolph, 117; Willi, 196.

[42]Ackroyd, *Chronicles,* 61.

[43]Ibid.

[44]Braun, "Significance," 228.

between this verse and the last chapter. 1 Chr 22:1 forms an apodosis to
the protasis of 1 Chr 21:28.[45]

> At that time, when David saw that the Lord had answered
> him at the threshing-floor of Ornan the Jebusite when he
> sacrificed there . . .

This means that vv 29-30 are a parenthetical aside discussing the holy
place at Gibeon. The chapter break after v 30 is unfortunate as it
obscures the true intention of the speech, which is to show the threshing-
floor of Ornan as the consecrated site of the temple as a result of Yahweh's revelation to David in response to the activities of Chap 21. Thus,
1 Chr 22:1 refers back to 1 Chr 21:28 and points forward as a rationale for
David's cultic preparations.

   Additional elements of the rationale are also present since there is no
specific audience mentioned and no immediate action results from the
speech.

   Clearly, this is a turning point in the narrative. The true temple site
has been revealed, over against Gibeon, as being in Jerusalem and David
can now proceed with the preparations for its construction. The Chronicler marks this turning point with a Royal Speech.

3. 1 Chr 23: [25-26, 28-32]

25. [For David said:
> The Lord, God of Israel, has given rest to his people; and
> he dwells in Jerusalem forever. 26. And so, the Levites
> no longer need to carry the tabernacle or any of the
> vessels for its service (27. for by the last words of David
> these were the number of the Levites from twenty years
> old and upward) 28. but their station shall be at the hand
> of the sons of Aaron for the service of the house of the
> Lord concerning the courts and the chambers and the
> purifying of every holy thing, and any work of the
> service of the house of God; 29. also for the showbread,
> the flour for the cereal offering, the wafers of unleav-
> ened bread, the baked offering, the offering mixed with
> oil and all measures of quantity or size. 30. And they
> shall stand every morning, to thank and praise the Lord,

---

[45]See W. E. Barnes, *The Books of Chronicles* (Cambridge: University
Press, 1899) 109; and Curtis, 254.

and likewise at evening. 31. Also to offer all burnt
offerings to the Lord, for the Sabbath, for the new
moons and set feasts, according to the number required
of them, continually before the Lord. 32. Thus shall they
keep charge of the tent of meeting and the sanctuary
and the sons of Aaron, their brothers, for the service of
the house of the Lord.]

There is some consensus that this material is not to be attributed to
the Chronicler.[46] H. G. M. Williamson states:

This is principally because on the one hand verses 6b-24 (with
the exception of the intrusive verses 13b-14) give a genealog-
ically related list of Levites who were to do the work for the
service of the house of the Lord (verse 24), thus correspond-
ing exactly with the context governed by xxiii 4, whereas, on
the other hand, verses 25-32 link together both this type of
Levite and the Levitical singers (verses 30-31), thereby
ignoring the distinctions made in verses 4-5, distinctions
which, moreover, the lists of 6b-24 and xxv 1-6 evidently
maintain.[47]

As in 1 Chr 15:2, the form of the introduction is suspicious as well and
supplements the weightier arguments cited above. The speech is, never-
theless, to be assigned to the group of rationales as there is no specific
audience addressed, and no imperatives or immediate action resulting
from the speech occurs. Rather, the speech gives a reason for the Levitical station as described in v 24.

4. 2 Chr 8:11a,[b]

Then Solomon brought Pharaoh's daughter up from the city
of David to the house which he had built for her, [for he
said:
My wife shall not dwell in the house of David, king of

---

[46]Willi, 203; Rudolph, 156; Noth, 112-114.

[47]H. G. M. Williamson, "The Origins of the Twenty-four Priestly
Courses, A Study of 1 Chronicles xxiii-xxvii," in *Studies in the Historical
Books of the Old Testament,* ed., J. A. Emerton (Leiden: E. J. Brill, 1979)
257-258. Williamson attributes the passage to a "pro-Priestly redactor" in
distinction to others.

> Israel, for the places to which the ark of the Lord has
> come are holy.]

The usual interpretation of this verse is concisely stated by Curtis:

> According to I K. 3:1 Solomon brought Pharaoh's daughter on
> her marriage into the city of David until the completion of
> the palace, when he made also a house for her (I K. 7:8), and
> according to I K. 9:24 she moved from the city of David into
> this house. The Chronicler passes over entirely the first
> statement and interprets the removal as caused by Solomon
> from a religious motive.[48]

This interpretation does explain the changes in the narrative portion of
the verse. However, it overlooks two features of Solomon's rationale that
are not congruent with the Chronicler's usual usage. First of all, the only
other Royal Speech that begins with the introductory formula כי אמר is
found at 1 Chr 23:25, which is generally attributed to a later expansion
and which is also a rationale dealing with cultic reasons for the taking of
a particular action. Secondly, the verb clearly shows the ark is here
thought of as feminine. Of the forty-nine occurrences of ארון in Chronicles, three do not refer to the ark of the covenant but to the "treasury
box";[49] thirty-four are ambiguous as there is no predicate or pronominal
suffix to indicate gender[50] and eleven are clearly masculine.[51] This is the
only reference in Chronicles that regards the ark as feminine.[52] For these
reasons, then, it seems best to regard 2 Chr 8:11a only, as being chronistic
and regarding Solomon's speech itself, as a probable expansion.

Braun, too, regards the speech as a rationale[53] though he considers it
to be chronistic. There are no imperatives, no specific audience is
addressed and no activity results from the speech, which gives the cultic
reason for Solomon's removal of his Egyptian wife.

---

[48]Curtis, 353.

[49]2 Chr 24:8, 10, 11.

[50]1 Chr 6:31; 13:3 (ו is ambiguous as it could also refer to God), 5, 6, 7,
9, 10, 12; 15:2, 14, 15, 23, 24, 25, 26, 27, 28; 16:4, 6, 37, 37; 17:1; 22:19;
28:2, 18; 2 Chr 5:2, 4, 5, 6, 9, 10; 6:11, 41; 35:3.

[51]1 Chr 13:13, 14; 15:1, 2, 3, 12, 29; 16:1; 2 Chr 1:4, 5:7, 8.

[52]The only other Old Testament reference to a feminine ark is 1 Sam
4:17.

[53]Braun, "Significance," 228.

5. 2 Chr 28:22b-23

The LXX has understood this verse in a variety of different ways. The MT reads:

> In the time of his distress he became yet more faithless to the Lord—this king Ahaz. For he sacrificed to the gods of Damascus which had defeated him, and said:
> > Because the gods of the kings of Syria helped them,
> > I will sacrifice to them that they may help me.

The LXX, however, reads:

> . . . but only troubled him in his affliction; and he departed yet more from the Lord, and the king said:
> > I will seek the gods of Damascus that strike me.
> And he said:
> > Because the gods of the king of Syria themselves strengthen them, therefore, I will sacrifice to them and they will help me.

For the unusual construction, "—this king Ahaz" (הוא המלך אחז) the LXX^{BA} has read, "and the king said" (καὶ εἶπεν ὁ βασιλεύς = אמר for אחז) while LXX^L adds the proper name Αχαζ.[54] In addition, the Greek has read, "I will seek" (LXX^{BA}: ἐκζητήσω, LXX^L: ζητήσω = אדרש) for the MT "and he sacrificed," and "me" for "him." Finally, we should read the Qal form עזרים for the Hiphil מעזרים the initial מ occurring due to dittography. At some point in the transmission of the text, a scribe has misread an original אמר as אחז, resulting in the received text. Thus, we will adopt the Greek text.

On either reading, the speech is clearly a rationale. Braun does not list 2 Chr 28:22-23 as a Royal Speech, so comparisons with his judgment cannot be made. However, there is no specific audience addressed, no imperatives are employed and Ahaz speaks to justify his cultic actions. It is noteworthy that this is the only Royal Speech delivered by a "bad king." The reasons for this will be discussed later.[55]

---

[54] BDB, 215e; and Curtis, 461 recognize this as "a late usage of the pronoun prefixed to the proper name for emphasis."

[55] See Chapter 7, below, where it will be shown that this, too, is a decisive turning point in the narrative.

This is the last Royal Speech to be grouped as a rationale. It was shown that these speeches are not directed to a specific audience, contain no imperatives and function as a means of justifying a particular cultic action rather than calling for a response, as in the edicts or the orations, to be examined below.

Orations

The descriptive formal characteristics of this group are as follows:

1. Designation of a specific audience

2. Use of imperatives or their equivalents to introduce the main points of the speech

3. Frequent use of historical retrospects either to the distant past or the immediate situation

As Braun has remarked, the distinction between this category and the category of edict is somewhat imprecise.[56] Several of the orations could be included in the category of edict. What seems to differentiate the orations is the frequent appearance of what will be called, for lack of a better term, historical retrospects. These may be in the classical form, which recalls the acts of God on behalf of his people (e.g., 2 Chr 30:7-8) but usually, they are merely allusions to events that have transpired in the distant or immediate past. Thus, those orations that clearly belong in the category will be examined first. Those orations that are less firmly anchored in the category will be discussed second.

1. 1 Chr 13:2-3

2. Then David said to all the assembly of Israel:
   If it seems good to you, (   )[57] let us send to our

---

[56]Braun, "Significance," 228.

[57]The translation of this part of the verse is difficult. The accentuation demands the conditional clause to end with "and from the Lord our God," making the נפרצה (Qal cohortative) the beginning of the next clause, parallel to נשלחה, and reading, "let us break out and send." This is possibly a pun on פרץ which occurs later in v 11 (Ackroyd, *Chronicles,* 57). Most commentators, following the Vulgate and LXX, read with Ehrlich

brothers who remain in all the lands of Israel and with
them the priests and the Levites in the cities of their
pasture lands [58] that they may gather to us. 3. Then let
us bring again the ark of our God to us; for we did not
seek it in the days of Saul.

This short speech begins with the Chronicler's characteristic framework
for Royal Speeches: ויאמר followed by the name of the king and the group
addressed. The main point of the speech is introduced by the cohortative
"let us send." This gathering of the remainder of the people, which
Ackroyd suggests may refer to "a later date when scattered communities
of Jews were to be found throughout the area, professing allegiance to
Jerusalem though living under separate political organizations,"[59] can
also be seen as portraying David's concern for the North in a proleptic
fashion. Hezekiah's summons for a Northern return in 2 Chr 30:6-9 is
possibly a reflection of this concern. A second point in the speech is again
introduced by a cohortative, "let us bring again." This time the emphasis
is upon the bringing in of the ark, which becomes the motif of chaps 13-
16. Thus, the speech is situated at a turning point in the narrative. A brief
historical retrospect contrasting the "days of Saul" concludes the speech.
In this instance, the action called for by the cohortatives is immediately
reported in the narrative (v 4) as in the edicts. The presence of the historical retrospect, however, makes this speech an oration.

2. 1 Chr 29:[1-5]

[1. Then David the king said to all the assembly:
Solomon, my son, whom alone God has chosen, is young
and inexperienced, but the work is great; for the palace
will not be for man but for the Lord God. 2. So, with all
my strength I have provided for the house of my God:
the gold for the things of gold, the silver for the things

נרצתה "acceptable" (εὐωδώθη) and connect this word to the conditional
clause: "and if it is acceptable to the Lord our God." Rudolph, 110, persuasively argues David could not have known the later reference to פרץ in
1 Chr 13:11, 14:11 and regards the clause to be a later gloss.

[58] Willi, 195, correctly sees this clause as a secondary addition due to
the appearance of מגרשים (cf. the other secondary occurrences, 1 Chr
5:11-17; 6:39-66; 2 Chr 11:14a; 31:12b-19, as well as, "die stilistisch
ungelenke Stellung des Umstandsatzes").

[59] Ackroyd, *Chronicles*, 57.

of silver, and the bronze for the things of bronze, the
iron for the things of iron, and wood for the things of
wood, stones of onyx, and settings, (antimony, variegated cloth and fine linen)[60] in abundance. 3. Moreover,
in addition to all that I have prepared for the holy
house, I have a treasure of my own of gold and silver,
and because of my devotion to the house of my God I
give it to the house of my God:[61] 4. three thousand
talents of gold, of the gold of Ophir, and seven thousand
talents of refined silver, for overlaying the walls of the
house[62] 5. (gold for the things of gold and silver for the
things of silver and the work to be done)[63] by craftsmen. Who then is willing to offer willingly[64] today for
the Lord?][65]

While this speech must be attributed to a later hand, as will be subsequently shown, it clearly belongs to the orations. The "assembly" is specifically addressed in v 1, the hortatory question of 5b functions as an
imperative asking for the assembly's response, and vv 2-5a are an historical retrospect of sorts, recalling David's generous contributions. In the
following vv (6-9) the people's response is related.

This speech does not occur at a turning point in the narrative, rather, it
interrupts the clear progression of events and even becomes the reason
for portraying the coronation of Solomon as a two day event (cf. v 21).[66]

---

[60]Curtis is surely correct in seeing כל אבן יקרה as a marginal gloss
explaining the unusual פור which was later inserted into the text after
הרקמה instead of before it. This would also account for the later insertion
of אבני before שיש making "fine linen" to read "stones of marble" as in
RSV. רקמה means "variegated cloth" in every other Old Testament reference except Ezek 17:3 (303).

[61]With RSV the order of the clauses needs to be rearranged to give a
clearer meaning.

[62]The MT has the plural. The singular occurs in LXX, Syriac, Vulgate
and Arabic.

[63]This phrase is lacking in the LXX and should probably be dropped.

[64]See the discussion in note 34, above.

[65]On the redactional character of the entire speech see Chapter 5,
below.

[66]These issues will be further examined in Chapter 5, below.

3. 2 Chr 2:2-9 (Eng 3-10)

2. Then Solomon sent to Huram the king of Tyre, saying:
As you dealt with David my father and sent him cedar
to build himself a house to dwell in, (so deal with me).[67]
3. Behold, I am about to build a house for the name of
the Lord, my God and dedicate it to him for the burning
of incense of sweet spices before him, and for the
continual offering of the showbread, and for burnt
offerings morning and evening, on the sabbaths and the
new moons and the appointed feasts of the Lord, our
God; this shall be upon Israel forever. 4. The house
which I am to build will be great, for our God is greater
than all gods. 5. But who is able to build him a house
since heaven, even the heaven of heavens cannot contain him? Who am I to build a house for him, except to
burn incense before him? 6. So now, send me a man
skilled to work in gold, silver, bronze and iron, in purple,
crimson and blue (fabrics), knowing how to engrave, to
be with the skilled men who are with me in Judah and
Jerusalem, whom David my father prepared. 7. Send me
also trees of cedar, cypress and algum from Lebanon,
for I know your servants know how to cut down the trees
of Lebanon; and behold my servants will be with your
servants, 8. to prepare timber for me in abundance, for
the house that I am to build will be wonderfully great.
9. And behold, I will give to the hewers, to those cutting
down the trees, twenty thousand cors of wheat for
food,[68] twenty thousand cors of barley, twenty thousand
baths of wine and twenty thousand baths of oil.

This speech is properly a letter send to Huram by Solomon through
couriers. 2 Chr 30:6-9 depicts Hezekiah sending a letter to the people of
Israel. However, the structure of the letter shows it to be similar to the
Chronicler's other orations: A specific audience is addressed, "Huram king

---

[67] This apodosis of the previous clause is lacking in the MT but seems to
be necessary for the sense. The Vulgate has supplied it with *sic fac
mecum*.

[68] חתים מכות "beaten wheat, wheat of the strokes" makes little sense as
the wheat would be threshed as a matter of course. Also, one would
expect the same adjective with the barley of the next clause. Therefore,
read with 1 Kgs 5:25, and others מַכֹּלֶת, see Rudolph, 200.

of Tyre" (v 2); an historical retrospect is employed to persuade Huram to
assist Solomon as he had helped David, (v 2); the main points of the speech
are introduced by the imperatives, "send me" (vv 6, 7) and the action
called for by the imperatives is reported in Huram's letter of reply (vv 10-
15).

It should also be noted that the particles עתה (v 6) and הנה (vv 3, 7, 9)
are used to provide structure and that the Chronicler's propensity for
rhetorical questions is again evidenced here in v 5.

Finally, the speech occurs at a turning point in the narrative. 2 Chr
1:18 (Eng 2:1) reads: "Now Solomon purposed to build a temple for the
name of the Lord . . ." Thus, the letter to Huram begins the account of
Solomon's preparations for the temple.[69]

4. 2 Chr 13:4-12

4. Then Abijah stood up on Mount Zemeriam which is in the
hill country of Ephriam and said:
Hear me, O Jeroboam and all Israel! 5. Do you not know
that the Lord, the God of Israel gave the kingship over
Israel forever to David and his sons by a covenant of
salt? 6. Yet, Jeroboam the son of Nebat, a servant of
Solomon the son of David, rose up and rebelled against
his lord;[70] 7. and certain worthless men gathered around
him, sons of Belial, and strengthened themselves against
Rehoboam the son of Solomon, because Rehoboam was
inexperienced and faint-hearted[71] and could not withstand them. 8. But now, you intend to resist the kingdom
of the Lord in the hand of David's sons because you are
a great army and have with you golden calves which
Jeroboam made you for gods. 9. Have you not driven out

---

[69]For the differences between this letter and the parallel in 1 Kgs 5:1-
6, 11, see 17f.
[70]The MT reads the plural which could possibly refer to Yahweh. The
versions, however, are unanimous in reading the singular.
[71]נער cannot mean "young" as is shown by 2 Chr 12:13 that gives Rehoboam's age as 41. "Inexperienced" seems better as in 1 Chr 22:5; 29:1;
1 Kgs 3:7. In a similar way רך-לבב "tender of heart" is either "timid" or
"weak in understanding" since לבב is the Hebrew equivalent for our
"mind." Of course, the portrayal of the revolt is quite different in the
speech from that of 2 Chr 10:1ff. which is based upon Kings. There,
Rehoboam is hard and defiant and brings on the revolt himself. Here, the
blame is laid upon the representatives of Israel, see Curtis, 375.

the priests the sons of Aaron, [and the Levites,][72] and made priests for yourselves from the people of the land?[73] Whoever comes to consecrate himself[74] with a young bull or seven rams becomes a priest of what are no gods. 10. But as for us, the Lord is our God, and we have not forsaken him; and priests minister to the Lord who are sons of Aaron [and the Levites are in his service[75]],[76] 11. for they offer to the Lord burnt offerings [and incense of sweet spices every morning and every evening, and the showbread is set upon the clean table as well as the golden lampstand with its lamps in order that it may burn every evening;][77] for we keep the charge of the Lord our God, but you have forsaken it. 12. Behold, God is with us at our head and his priests with the signal trumpets to sound the battle call against you. O sons of Israel, do not fight against the Lord, the God of your fathers, for you cannot succeed.

Abijah's speech is the parade example of the Chronicler's orations and literally teems with his theological themes. A specific audience, "Jeroboam and all Israel" is designated in v 4, although the real addressees are "all Israel" alone as shown by the references to Jeroboam in the third person in vv 6, 7, 8 and the vocative of v 12. Two historical retrospects occur, one with reference to Israel (vv 5-7, 9) and one with reference to Judah (vv 10, 11). The main point of the address, Abijah's plea to Israel to stop fighting against Yahweh, is introduced by the jussive with אל "do not fight" in v 12. At the beginning of the address, the imperative sentence שמעוני appears for the first time in the speeches we have examined. Apart from Gen 23:8, which is not a speech, this imperative introduction

---

[72]On the redactional character of the phrase, see Willi, 197.

[73]RSV translates the MT as, "like the peoples of other lands." The Greek has a better contrast, ἐκ τοῦ λαοῦ τῆς γῆς, and fits better with 1 Kgs 12:31, see Curtis, 376.

[74]Literally, "to fill his hand," here used in the technical sense of becoming a priest.

[75]Reading בְּמֶלַאכְתּוֹ since the phrase only occurs in construct and the word is in pause here, the final ו has dropped out due to haplography with the initial ו of the next word, see Ehrlich, 361.

[76]On the redactional character, see Willi, 197.

[77]Ibid.; as well as Adolf Büchler, "Zur Geschichte der Tempelmusik und der Tempelpsalmen," ZAW 19 (1899) 99.

only occurs in Chronicles and usually in the Royal Orations.[78] The actions called for by the imperatives or their equivalents are reported in the narrative (vv 13-19) although, in this case, they are of a negative character. Israel did not desist from fighting but set an ambush that failed to succeed.

Once again, the speech occurs at a turning point in the narrative. It will be, argued in Chapter 7 that Abijah's speech introduced the Chronicler's second major division in the history of the monarchy.

5. 2 Chr 14:6 (Eng 7)

> Then he said to Judah:
> Let us build these cities and surround them by walls and towers, gates and a bar,[79] (while we are master of the land.)[80] (For as)[81] we have sought the Lord, our God, he has sought us)[82] and given us rest on every side.
> So they built and prospered.[83]

Asa's brief speech is short enough to be considered an edict were it not for the historical retrospect. A specific audience is addressed ("Judah") and the cohortative "let us build" introduces the speech. The response of the addressees to the cohortative is described in the final clause.

After the war with Israel under Abijah, Judah was now enjoying the rest Yahweh had provided (vv 1b, 6b). The Chronicler has used this period (vv 2-6a) to describe his elaborations of Asa's reforms (from 1 Kgs 15:9-15) in a more explicit fashion. Following the speech, there is war once again, this time with Zerah the Ethiopian, which is not mentioned in Kings. As the speech both culminates the peaceful years and provides the

---

[78]1 Chr 28:2; 2 Chr 13:4; 20:20; 29:5. 2 Chr 15:2 and 28:11 are prophetic speeches.

[79]Reading וברית for the plural since the expression is דלתים ובריח in 2 Chr 8:5; Deut 3:5; 1 Sam 23:7.

[80]Based on Rudolph's paraphrase of the LXX ἐν ᾧ τῆς γῆς κυριεύσο-μεν this gives a better sense than the RSV, "the land is still ours," (240).

[81]Again, adopting the LXX ὅτι καθῶς = כְּדָרְשֵׁנוּ for כִּי דָרַשְׁנוּ gives better sense (ibid.).

[82]Again, reading with LXX ἐξεζήτησαν ἡμας = דְּרָשָׁנוּ for דָּרַשְׁנוּ eliminates the unnecessary repetition of "we have sought" especially since one would expect "him" following the MT (ibid.).

[83]This time, the LXX καὶ εὐόδωσεν ἡμιν = וְלָנוּ הִצְלִיחַ "and he prospered us," should not be accepted as it would eliminate the people's response to Asa's speech (contra Rudolph, ibid.).

backdrop for the holy war of vv 9-14, it may be seen as occurring at a turning point in the narrative.

6. 2 Chr 29:3-11

3. In the first year of his reign, in the first month, he opened the doors of the house of the Lord, and repaired them. 4. He brought in the priests and the Levites, and gathered them in the square on the east, 5. and said to them:

> Hear me, O Levites![84] Now sanctify yourselves, and sanctify the house of the Lord, the God of your fathers, and carry out the filth from the sanctuary. 6. For our fathers have been unfaithful and have done evil in the sight of the Lord, our God; they have forsaken him and turned their faces away from the dwelling place of the Lord, and turned their backs. 7. They have also shut the doors of the porch and extinguished the lamps, and have not burned incense or offered burnt offerings in the sanctuary to the God of Israel. 8. Therefore, the wrath of the Lord was upon Judah and Jerusalem, and he has made them an object of horror, of astonishment and of hissing, as you see with your own eyes. 9. For behold, our fathers have fallen by the sword and our sons and our daughters and our wives are in captivity for this. 10. Now, it is in my heart to make a covenant with the Lord, the God of Israel, that his burning anger may turn away from us. 11. My sons, do not be negligent[85] now, for the Lord has chosen you to stand before him, to minister to him and to be his ministers and burn incense.

Hezekiah's straightforward speech is addressed to a specific audience ("the priests and the Levites" v 4; the generic "Levites" v 5), employs imperatives to introduce the major purpose of the speech (the two-fold "sanctify" and "carry out" of v 5 as well as the concluding "be not negligent" of v 11), and an historical retrospect is contained in vv 6-9. Furthermore, with the omission of the redactional vv 12-15, the action

---

[84]That the term must be seen as including the priests is shown by the priests' response in vv 16ff. Willi, 199, sees vv 12-15, which describe the activity of the Levites, as redactional (contra Rudolph, 293) because the priests and Levites are not pictured as part of the same group.

[85]שׁלה only occurs here in the Niphal. Ehrlich (375) suggests reading תֵּרָשְׁלוּ since the Hithpael of רשׁל has this meaning in modern Hebrew.

called for by the imperatives is performed by the addressees in vv 16-17. The logical flow of the oration is shown by the literary use of הנה (v 9, as the conclusion of the retrospect) and עתה (v 10, as the introduction of Hezekiah's proposed solution to the problem of the previous unfaithfulness).

Since the oration introduces the major contribution of Hezekiah, the reunification of the North and the South by means of the combined Passover, it may be seen as occurring at a turning point in the narrative.

7. 2 Chr 30:4-9

4. Therefore, since the plan pleased the king and all the assembly, 5. they established a decree that a proclamation should pass through all Israel, from Beersheba to Dan, to come, to celebrate a Passover to the Lord, the God of Israel, at Jerusalem, because they had not celebrated together[86] as it is written. 6. So, runners, with letters from the hand of the king and his officials went through all Israel and Judah, according to the hand of the king,[87] saying:

> O Israelites, return to the Lord, the God of Abraham, Isaac and Israel, that he may return to your remnant who have escaped from the hand of the kings of Assyria. 7. Do not be like your fathers and your brothers who were faithless to the Lord, the God of their fathers, so that he gave them up to horror, as you see. 8. Now, do not stiffen your necks like your fathers, but submit to the Lord, come to his sanctuary, which he has sanctified forever and serve the Lord your God, in order that his fierce anger may turn from you. 9. For when you return to the Lord, your brothers and your sons will be merci-

---

[86]The meaning of לרב is uncertain. Most translate "in great numbers" but others (Luther, DeWette) as "for a long time." Since the temporal meaning is not attested, and v 24 reads לרב with reference to the multitude while v 26 refers to the length of time that has passed, we read with Myers, *II Chronicles,* 173 "en masse."

[87]Since the clause lacks a verb, and the runners only go to the North (v 6b), while they were sent to "all Israel and Judah," (v 6a), Rudolph claims the clause is incomplete and inserts "and according to the command of the king: 'Speak to the Israelites in the name of the king, saying,'" after וכמצות המלך, which has fallen out by homoioteleuton (300). We simply drop the ו on וכמצות with 1 MS., LXX and Vulgate.

> fully dealt with by their captors and allowed to return[88]
> to this land, for the Lord, your God, is gracious and
> merciful and will not turn his face from you, if you
> return to him.

Hezekiah's summons for a united Passover contains all the elements normally found in the Chronicler's orations. A specific audience is addressed "O Israelites" (v 6); four imperatives ("return" v 6, "yield," "enter," "serve" v 8) and two jussives ("be not like" v 7, "stiffen not" v 8) provide access to the main points of the address; an historical retrospect is found in vv 7-8 and the people respond to the imperatives in vv 10-12 of the narrative framework. The Northerners respond both negatively (v 10) and positively (v 11), while the Southerners are moved by God to respond affirmatively (v 12).

This speech, by forming a parenthesis with Abijah's similar summons to the North for a return to Jerusalem, encloses the second portion of the Chronicler's periodization of history: the Divided Monarchy.[89] As such it occurs at a dramatic point in the narrative. Hezekiah's speech inaugurates the activites that will eventually culminate in the combined Passover that will be celebrated by both North and South in 2 Chr 30:13-27.

The previous speeches are all structurally similar and may be classified as orations. They address a specific audience, introduce their main point by means of imperatives or equivalents, contain historical retrospects and report the audience as acting upon the imperatives in the subsequent narrative. The following speeches, while still to be classified as orations, do not fulfill all these requirements and thus could possibly be simply edicts. They will be translated and discussed with this in mind.

1. 2 Chr 32:6-8

> 6. Then he set military officers over the people and gathered
> them to him in the square at the gate of the city and spoke
> encouragingly to them, saying:
>> 7. Be strong and courageous, fear not and be not dis-
>> mayed before the king of Assyria and all the army that

---

[88] The verb is understood with the plural לרחמים as its object as shown by the addition of ל. Thus, the infinitive construct ולשוב is attached to the understood verb by the ו, continuing its action, see Emil Kautsch, ed., *GKC* (Oxford: Oxford University Press, 1910) #114p.

[89] See Chapter 7, below.

> is with him; for (the one) with us is greater than (the
> one) with him. 8. With him is an arm of flesh, but with
> us is the Lord, our God, to help us and fight our battles.
> And the people were supported by the words of Hezekiah
> king of Judah.

Hezekiah's words of encouragement in the face of Sennacherib's invasion also contain the elements of the orations. A specific audience is
gathered and addressed ("the military officers and people," v 6); the four-
fold formula of encouragement is quoted from Deut 31:6, Josh 10:25 and
1 Chr 22:13, 28:20 and employs the imperatives "Be strong, be courageous" and the jussives "fear not, be not dismayed" (v 7) to introduce this
main point of the speech. The theme of reliance upon Yahweh that is so
prominent in the prayers of Chronicles is lifted up in a paraphrase of Jer
17:5 ("an arm of flesh" v 8). In v 8b the people are reported as responding
positively, to the imperatives, in the narrative framework.

This speech occurs at a crucial point in the narrative, the invasion of
the re-united monarchy by external forces. The Chronicler means to show
by this speech that all will be well if the people rely solely upon God.

2. 1 Chr 22:7-13 [14-16, 17-19]

> 7. David said to Solomon, his son:[90]
>> As for me, it was in my heart to build a house for the
>> name of the Lord my God. 8. But, the word of the Lord
>> came to me saying:
>>> You have spilled much blood and waged great wars;
>>> you shall not build a house for my name, because you
>>> have spilled so much blood on the ground before me.
>>> 9. Behold, a son shall be born to you; he shall be a
>>> man of rest. I will give him rest from all his enemies
>>> round about, for Solomon shall be his name, and I will
>>> give peace and quiet to Israel in his days. 10. He will
>>> build a house for my name, and I will become his

---

[90]Reading the Kethib against the Qere (בני "My son,") and the versions. Braun draws our attention to the usage in 1 Chr 28:6; 29:1 and
28:20, the beginning of direct discourse, ("Significance," 14). Furthermore,
אני usually stands first after the designation of the audience, except in
1 Chr 29:2, which is secondary. Also, the designation "Solomon, his son"
occurs in the previous verse. These arguments are weakened, however, by
the address of בני in v 11.

father, and I will establish the throne of his reign over Israel forever.

11. Now, my son, the Lord be with you that you may be successful and build the house of the Lord your God, as he has spoken concerning you. 12. Only, may the Lord give you discretion and understanding to command[91] Israel, so that you may keep the law of the Lord your God. 13. Then you will prosper, if you are careful to observe the statutes and the ordinances which the Lord commanded Moses for Israel. Be strong and courageous, fear not and be not dismayed. [14. Now, behold, with great pains I have prepared for the house of the Lord 100,000 talents of gold and 1,000,000 talents of silver, and bronze and iron beyond weight, because there is so much of it. I have also prepared timber and stone, but you must add to them. 15. You have an abundance of workmen: stonecutters, masons, carpenters, and all kinds of craftsmen without number, skilled in working 16. gold, silver, bronze and iron. Arise and work, and may the Lord be with you.][92]

[17. David also commanded all the leaders of Israel to help Solomon his son, saying:

18. Is not the Lord, your God with you? And has he not given you rest on every side? For he has given the

---

[91] The MT: וִיצַוְּךָ עַל "and may he give you command over," as well as the LXX: κατισκύσαι "he will strengthen you" are impossible here, as they cannot be translated as wishes since the fulfillment of the promise has already taken place in 9ff. Therefore, we must adopt Ehrlich's conjecture and read אֶת גֻּלְצֹ'ת (348-349). Others, to retain the text, consider וִיצוֹר as initiating a temporal clause and translate "when he gives you charge over Israel. . . ."

[92] This long expansion is usually taken to be the Chronicler's. Rudolph's reasons for seeing it as redactional are: (1) the high figures employed do not tally with other such lists in Chronicles such as 2 Chr 9:13. (2) David's placing workmen at Solomon's disposal is a heightening of v 12. (3) v 13 forms a clear conclusion (151). Braun has provided additional evidence: (1) v 14 with והנה provides only a loose connection after the preceding והנה (2) The disjointed character of the material: a) v 14, כי לרב היה, the author forgets he is quoting David in the present tense. b) v 16, repeats the gold, silver, bronze and iron of v 14 and says they are "without number" although he has just described them quantitatively in v 14. c) vv 2-4 make no mention of workmen other than masons, no gold and no silver ("Significance," 16).

> dwellers of the land into my hand and the land is sub-
> dued before the Lord and before his people. 19. Now, set
> your mind and heart to seek the Lord your God. Arise
> and build the sanctuary of the Lord God, so that you
> may bring the ark of the covenant of the Lord and the
> holy vessels of God into the house that is to be built for
> the name of the Lord.] [93]

Examination of the Chronicler's material (1 Chr 22:7-13) shows the speech to be like the other orations in that it begins with a specific desig- nation of audience ("Solomon, his son," v 7), makes use of imperatives ("be strong, be courageous, fear not, be not dismayed" v 13) as the main point of the speech, employs an historical retrospect in the form of Yahweh's speech (vv 8-10) and David's remembering of his intentions (v 7).

It differs from the other orations we have seen in that the narrative does not immediately report Solomon's carrying out of the imperatives. This can be explained when it is remembered that chaps 23-27 are an insertion that seems to separate David's private and public addresses in chaps 22, 28, and 29. Solomon could not begin to act upon the directives of his father until after the coronation which takes place in chap 29. 1 Chr 29:33 which occurs immediately after the coronation relates:

> Then Solomon sat on the throne of the Lord as king instead of
> his father David; and he prospered (צלח) and all Israel obeyed
> (שמע) him.

That David's charge to Solomon to build the temple is a key point in the narrative is clear.

---

[93]While most see this section as a later expansion (Rudolph, 101-102; Noth, 112), Braun points out this is usually because it appears to be a doublet of Chapter 28. But there is no indication of a prior convening of the leaders (cf., v 17) and there is no reason to assume they were present for David's address to Solomon. Furthermore, Chapter 18 only asks the assembly to help Solomon by defraying the cost through an offering. Therefore, the insertion of this address to the leaders was due to the great insertion of 1 Chr 23-27, which made David's private address (1 Chr 22) and public address (1 Chr 28) appear to be separated ("Significance," 41).

> 3. *1 Chr 28:2-3, [4-6a], 6b-7, [8], 9-12a,*
> *[12b-13a], 13b, [14-18], 19-20, [21a], 21b*

2. Then King David rose to his feet and said:
    Hear me, my brothers and my people. As for me, I had it
    in my heart to build a house of rest for the ark of the
    covenant of the Lord and for the footstool of our God;
    and I made preparations for building. 3. But God said to
    me:
    > You shall not build a house for my name because you
    > are a man of war and have shed blood.

    4. [Yet, the Lord, the God of Israel, chose me from all
    the house of my father to be king over Israel forever.
    For he has chosen Judah to be a leader; and in the house
    of Judah, my father's house, and among the sons of my
    father he took pleasure in me to make me king over all
    Israel. 5. And of all my sons, for the Lord has given me
    many sons, he has chosen Solomon, my son, to sit on the
    throne of the kingdom of the Lord over Israel. 6. And he
    said to me:][94]
    > Your son Solomon is the one who shall build my house
    > and my courts; for I have chosen him to be my son,
    > and I will be his father. 7. I will establish his kingdom
    > forever, if he resolutely performs my commandments
    > and my ordinances as he is today.

    [8. So now, in the sight of all Israel, the assembly of the
    Lord, and in the hearing of our God, observe and seek
    after all the commandments of the Lord your God in
    order that you may possess the good land and bequeath
    it to your sons after you forever.][95] 9. And now,[96]

---

[94]Braun has persuasively argued this insertion to be an expansion of the
concept of election in vv 6, 10; since it interrupts the Yahweh speech of
vv 3, 6; since its concern is with Solomon as king and not as temple
builder as in the rest of the speech; and also, since the idea of Judah's
election is unprecedented in Chronicles ("Significance," 41.)

[95]This verse, too, is a later expansion as shown by the plural verb
forms in a speech directed to Solomon, and the idea of "bequeathing the
land" which is otherwise foreign in Chronicles, as well as the discrepancies in LXX[B] (ibid. 42). Further evidence for the secondary character of
v 8 is the unique construct relationship of קהל יהוה.

[96]Reading ועתה with the LXX and not ואתה "and as for you." As Braun
observes, "With the addition of v 8 with its introductory weʿattâ the
identical form at the beginning of v 9 was altered" (ibid., 42).

Solomon my son, know the God of your fathers[97] and
serve him with a whole heart and with a willing mind;
for the Lord searches all hearts, and understands every
plan and thought. If you seek him, he will be found by
you; but if you forsake him, he will reject you forever.
10. Consider, now, for the Lord has chosen you to build
a house for the sanctuary; be strong and do it.

11. Then David gave to Solomon his son the pattern of the
porch and its houses, its treasuries, its upper rooms and its
inner chambers, and of the room for the mercy seat;
12. and the pattern of all that he had in mind for the
course of the house of the Lord and for all the surrounding
rooms; [for the store houses . . .][98] and for all the vessels
for the service in the house of the Lord. [the weight of
gold for all golden vessels . . .][99] 19. All (this) he made
clear to him in a writing from the hand of the Lord.[100]
20. Then David said to Solomon his son:

Be strong and courageous and do it, fear not and be not
dismayed; for the Lord God, even my God, is with you.
He will not fail you or forsake you until all the work for
the service of the house of the Lord is finished.[101]
[21. And behold the divisions of the priests and the

---

[97]Plural with the LXX.

[98]Vv 12b-13a are redactional; see Rudolph, 185; accepted by Willi, 196;
and Braun, "Significance," 44.

[99]Vv 14-18 are another expansion; see Rudolph, ibid.; and Willi, ibid.
Braun, who recognizes the expansion in vv 14-18, chooses to delete v 13b
as well (ibid.). But the arguments against the longer expansions deal with
their specificity. Thus, we retain v 13b with Rudolph and Willi.

[100]The exact text and wording of v 19 is unclear since the Hebrew
suddenly shifts to the first person, literally, "All this was in writing from
the hand of Yahweh; he caused me (עלי) to understand all the works of the
pattern." RSV alters עלי to עליו and transposes the athnach under it,
translating, "All . . . concerning it, all the work . . ." Braun, however,
suggests the subject of השכיל may be David, not Yahweh and alters עלי to
עליו which must be done anyway, and reads with the LXX ἔδωκεν Δαωειδ
Σαλωμων "David gave Solomon" with עליו referring to Solomon, this allows
one textual change and avoids the problems associated with "the writing
from the hand of Yahweh" that usually arise in this verse (ibid., 44).

[101]The repetition of vv 11-12a following v 20 in the LXX is
"textkritisch bedeutungslos," Rudolph, 188.

Levites for all the service of the house of God][102] And
with you in all the work will be every willing man who
has skill for any kind of service; also the officers and all
the people will be wholly at your command.

Like the preceding speech, David's speech to the assembly in Jerusalem
displays many of the characteristics of the orations. It is specifically
addressed to "my brothers and my people," (v 2) and "Solomon," (v 9). It
uses many imperatives to direct us to the emphases of the speech, "know,"
"serve" (v 9); "consider," "be strong," "do it" (v 10); "be strong," "be courageous," "fear not," "do it," "be not dismayed" (v 20). There is an historical
retrospect contained in vv 2-3, 6b-7, which explains why David is exhort-
ing his son to build the temple. Also like the previous speech, the narrative does not immediately report Solomon's acting upon the directives of
his father; again, this is due to the fact that he first must be crowned.

Finally, the speech occurs at a key point in the narrative, the presentation and justification of Solomon to the people as God's chosen king and
temple-builder. As is well known, the Chronicler omits all the events of
the so-called "Succession Narrative" in Dtr in order to justify Solomon as
Yahweh's chosen temple-builder and to solidify the unity of his reign with
that of his father.

3. 2 Chr 19:4-11

4. Jehoshaphat lived in Jerusalem but he went out again
among the people from Beersheba to the hill country of
Ephraim in order to bring them back to the Lord, the God
of their fathers. 5. He appointed judges in the land in all
the fortified cities of Judah, city by city, 6. and said to the
judges:
    Consider what you are about to do, for you shall judge
    not for man but for the Lord; he[103] is with you in the
    matter of judgment. 7. Now, then, let the fear of the
    Lord be upon you, be careful and do, for there is no

---

[102]V 21a is redactional, ibid., 190.

[103]Grammatically, the clause lacks a subject. While this is not unusual
for the Chronicler (cf., Arno Kropat, *Die Syntax des Autors der Chronik
vergleichen mit der seiner Quellen* [Giessen: Alfred Töpelmann, 1909] 63-
64), "he" has probably fallen out of the text by haplography (Rudolph,
256).

perversity with the Lord, our God, nor partiality, nor
taking of a bribe.

8. Moreover, in Jerusalem, Jehoshaphat appointed some of
[the Levites and][104] the priests and some of the heads of
the fathers' of Israel for the judgments of the Lord (and for
the controversies of the inhabitants of Jerusalem).[105]
9. Then he charged them, saying:
Thus you shall do in the fear of the Lord, faithfully and
wholeheartedly: 10. whenever a controversy comes to
you from your brothers who live in their cities, concerning [murder or manslaughter],[106] law or commandment,
statutes or ordinances, then you shall warn[107] them,
that they may not be guilty before the Lord and that
wrath may (not) come upon you and your brothers. Thus
you shall do and you will not be guilty. 11. Behold,
Amaraiah the chief priest will be over you in all matters
of the Lord; and Zebadiah, the son of Ishmael, the
governor of the house of Judah, in all matters of the
king. [Also, the Levites will be officers before you.][108]
Be strong and act, and may the Lord be with the good.

The speeches of Jehoshaphat, here and in 2 Chr 20:20, to be examined
next, do not fit as neatly into our categories as the Chronicler's other
speeches. Specific audiences are addressed ("The judges" in v 6 and "some
of the priests and heads of the fathers' house" in v 8), and imperatives
("Consider" v 6, "be careful and do" v 7, "Be strong and act" v 11) and
jussives ("let the fear of Yahweh be upon you" v 7) summarize the main
points of the exhortation, but there are no historical retrospects, unless

---

[104]The placement of "the Levite" *before* the priests is quite at odds
with the Chronicler's usual practice. The LXX has corrected this unusual
construction by placing "the Levites" after "the priests." It is best,
however, to regard "the Levites and" as a later addition with Willi, 198.

[105]The MT reads, "disputes. And they returned (וַיָּשֻׁבוּ) to Jerusalem."
But שוב means "to return" and gives no sense. RSV has read, "They had
their seat (וַיֵּשְׁבוּ) in Jerusalem." Our translation reflects the reading of
the versions (LXX and Vulgate) וּלְרִיבֵי יֹשְׁבֵי as in Curtis, 404; and
Rudolph, 256.

[106]Literally, "between blood and blood," i.e., a decision between one
kind of bloodshed and another as in Deut 17:8, Exod 21:12-14.

[107]Not "instruct" as in RSV, cf., *BDB*, 264.

[108]Another secondary expansion, lacking in several LXX MSS, see
Willi, 198 and note 105, above.

one would want to take the strong Deuteronomic coloring of the passage as reminiscent of the earlier times,[109] and there is no description of the addressees response to the imperatives in the subsequent narrative. This last point would seem to exclude 2 Chr 19:6f, 9-11 from the category of edict as well.

With these reservations, then, Jehoshaphat's commissioning of the judges will be classified as one of the orations, with Braun.[110]

This imprecise classification does not alter the fact that this speech occurs at a turning point in the narrative, however. The Chronicler takes great pains to idealize Jehoshaphat over against the picture presented in Kings. The Kings account, which only records the campaigns of Jehoshaphat with Ahab (1 Kings 22, 2 Chronicles 18) and with Jehoram and the king of Edom (2 Kings 3, no parallel), is overly concerned with Jehoshaphat's contemporary, Ahab of Israel, and the prophets Elijah and Elisha. But Jehoshaphat is important for the Chronicler. Therefore, he records 1 Kgs 22:43, that Jehoshaphat followed his father Asa in obedience to the cult (2 Chr 20:32f) and was rewarded for consciously emulating the Davidic ideal (2 Chr 17:3ff) with peace and prosperity (2 Chr 17:10ff). This speech and 2 Chr 20:20, to be discussed below, function then, as examples of Jehoshaphat's faith and favor with God.

If there is "no real basis for ascribing historicity to the present account,"[111] Jehoshaphat's reform may be seen as an idealization based upon his name "Yahweh is judge" as Wellhausen posited earlier.[112] In any case, the speech is crucially located.

---

[109]Cf., Deut 16:18-20; 17:8-13; and see Ackroyd, *Chronicles*, 146.

[110]"Significance," 228. Braun notices the different character of this speech with regard to contents as well. He posits two classifications, speeches concerned with cultic places and objects, especially the temple, and speeches made to the troops before battle. Only Jehoshaphat's judicial reform does not fit either category (ibid., 230-231).

[111]Ackroyd, *Chronicles*, 146. Willi, too, expresses doubt about the historicity of the reform, 197-198. Positive conclusions are reached by W. F. Albright, "The Judicial Reform of Jehoshaphat (2 Chr 19:5-11)," in *Alexander Marx Jubilee Volume*, English Section (New York, 1950) 61-82; Frank M. Cross and George E. Wright, "The Boundary and Province Lists of the Kingdom of Judah," *JBL* 75 (1956) 202-226; and Myers, *II Chronicles*, 108-109.

[112]Wellhausen, 191.

4. 2 Chr 20:20

And they rose early in the morning and went out to the wilderness of Tekoa; and as they went out, Jehoshaphat stood and said:

> Hear me, Judah and the inhabitants of Jerusalem! Believe in the Lord, your God and you will be established; believe his prophets and you will succeed.

This second speech of Jehoshaphat presents problems of classification similar to those in his first speech to the judges. A definite audience is addressed ("Judah and the inhabitants of Jerusalem"). But, unless one chooses to take the paraphrase of Isa 7:9 as an historical retrospect, there are no historical retrospects and no narrative description of the people's response. Once again, this last point precludes assigning the speech to the category of edict, and it seems best to classify it as an oration with an implied description of response.

Jehoshaphat's speech serves as a further example of his piety as did his judicial reform. Furthermore, it will be shown in Chapter 7 that it sets the tone of the Chronicler's entire second period of history, the Divided Monarchy. As such, its placement in the narrative is significant.

III. SUMMARY

It has been shown that the orations are to be distinguished from the rationales in that they address a specific audience, employ imperatives or their equivalents to introduce the major concern of the speech and usually report the addressees' response to the imperative in the narrative framework. The orations are to be distinguished from the edicts in that they are usually longer, make use of equivalents for the edict's imperative and generally contain historical retrospects to make their point. Furthermore, it has been demonstrated that the Royal Speeches do occur at turning points in the narrative (contra Noth) and thus may be used to determine the structural framework of the Chronicler's work. It is the contention of this dissertation that once the Chronicler's structure has been determined his theological presuppositions and message will become evident, as will be shown in Chapter 7.

3

Royal Prayer in Chronicles

J. M. Myers has remarked concerning the Chronicler's prayer in general that, "prayer was accentuated in the work of the Deuteronomist; it is also evident in that of the Chronicler. In fact it seems to be stressed even more by him. . . ."[1] As far as it goes, this opinion is surely true. However, it is the contention of this study that this accentuation of prayer is most clearly discernible and most profitably employed for the investigation of the structure and theology of Chronicles in the sub-category of *Royal* Prayer, those prayers composed by the Chronicler and placed on the lips of the kings. Consequently, the first task of this chapter will be to determine which prayers constitute the category of Royal Prayers and of those so determined, which prayers are most likely to contain the Chronicler's own distinctive thought. The second task will be to analyze the Chronicler's Royal Prayers in a more detailed manner as to translation and text, and finally to make some observations on their form-critical nature.

I. DETERMINATION OF THE CHRONICLER'S ROYAL PRAYER

To determine the Chronicler's Royal Prayers, a set of criteria, similar to those devised in the last chapter for determining the Chronicler's Royal Speeches, will be employed. They are as follows:

1. The prayer is on the lips of the king

2. The prayer is reported in direct discourse

3. The prayer is unique to Chronicles

---

[1] Myers, *I Chronicles,* lxvi.

4. The prayer, though paralleled in the *Vorlage*, has been significantly altered

On the basis of criterion 1, all prayers such as that of Jabez (1 Chr 4:9-10) where the petitioner is not a king, may be eliminated from consideration. On the basis of criterion 2, such references to kings praying as 2 Chr 33:12f where the Chronicler reports Manasseh as praying to God but does not quote in direct discourse the words of the king, may be eliminated. This leaves ten instances of Royal Prayer in Chronicles that fulfill the requirements of the first two criteria.[2] Of these ten, four (1 Chr 29:10-19; 2 Chr 14:10; 20:6-12; 38:18f) have no parallel in the books of Samuel-Kings and may be assumed to contain the Chronicler's own thought on the basis of criterion 3. These will be taken up below in the discussion of text, translation and structure. At this time it is necessary to compare the remaining six prayers with their parallels in Dtr to see if the Chronicler has made them his own in any significant way.

1. 1 Chr 14:10a = 2 Sam 5:19a

	2 Samuel	1 Chronicles
a	וַיִּשְׁאַל דָּוִד בַּיהוָה לֵאמֹר	וַיִּשְׁאַל דָּוִיד בֵּאלֹהִים לֵאמֹר
b	הַאֶעֱלֶה אֶל־פְּלִשְׁתִּים	הַאֶעֱלֶה עַל־פְּלִשְׁתִּיים
c	הֲתִתְּנֵם בְּיָדִי	וּנְתַתָּם בִּידִי

In this brief prayer only minor orthographic and linguistic alterations can be observed. The *plene* spelling of "David" (line a), the curious spelling of "Philistines" (line b), the substitution of "God" for "Yahweh" (line a) and על for אל (line b) as well as the use of the Qal perfect of נתן for the Qal imperfect with ה interrogative (line c), involve no theological transformations.

---

[2] 1 Chr 14:10a = 2 Sam 5:19a; 17:16-27 = 7:17-29; 21:8 = 24:10; 21:17 = 24:17; 29:10-19; 2 Chr 1:8-10 = 1 Kgs 3:6-9; 6:14-42 = 8:23-53; 14:10; 20:6-12; 30:18-19.

2. 1 Chr 21:8 = 2 Sam 24:10

	2 Samuel	1 Chronicles
a	וַיֹּאמֶר דָּוִד אֶל־יְהוָה חָטָאתִי מְאֹד	ויאמר דָּוִיד אֶל־הָאֱלֹהִים חטאתי מאד
b	אֲשֶׁר עָשִׂיתִי	אשר עשיתי אֶת־הַדָּבָר הַזֶּה
c	וְעַתָּה יְהוָה הַעֲבֶר־נָא	ועתה העבר־נא
d	אֶת־עֲוֹן עַבְדְּךָ	אֶת־עֲווֹן עבדך
e	כִּי נִסְכַּלְתִּי מְאֹד	כי נסכלתי מאד

In this prayer as well only minor orthographic and linguistic changes
appear. Besides the usual *plene* spelling of "David" (line a) and the substitution of "God" for "Yahweh" (line a), the Chronicler offers the *plene*
spelling of עוון (line d), omits the vocative "O Yahweh" (line c), and adds
the epexegetic "in this matter" (line b). Again, no theological motives are
in evidence.

3. 1 Chr 21:17 = 2 Sam 24:17

	2 Samuel	1 Chronicles
a	וַיֹּאמֶר דָּוִד אֶל־יְהוָה	ויאמר דָּוִיד אֶל־הָאֱלֹהִים
b	בִּרְאֹתוֹ אֶת־הַמַּלְאָךְ הַמַּכֶּה בָעָם	
c	וַיֹּאמֶר	
d		הֲלֹא אֲנִי אָמַרְתִּי לִמְנוֹת בָּעָם
e	הִנֵּה אָנֹכִי חָטָאתִי	וַאֲנִי־הוּא אֲשֶׁר־חטאתי
f	וְאָנֹכִי הֶעֱוֵיתִי	וְהָרֵעַ הֲרֵעוֹתִי
g	וְאֵלֶּה הַצֹּאן מֶה עָשׂוּ	ואלה הצאן מה עשו
h	תְּהִי נָא יָדְךָ	יְהוָה אֱלֹהַי תהי נא ידך
i	בִּי וּבְבֵית אָבִי	בי ובבית אבי
j		וּבְעַמְּךָ לֹא לְמַגֵּפָה

The text of Samuel is quite corrupt in this section. New evidence from
4QSam[a] has established conclusively that 1 Chr 21:16 preceded 2 Sam

14:17.[3] This has led F. M. Cross to conclude that the fuller text of 1 Chr 21:16 provides "an alternative to the words 'When David saw the angel who was striking the people,'" (line b).[4] If this is the case, one might also posit an original Samuel reading that included the 1 Chr 21:17 (line d) reading above that has dropped out due to haplography (homoioteleuton בעם), and a subsequent haplography (homoioteleuton בעם), this time on the part of the Chronicler (or the scribal tradition), of 1 Sam 24:17 (line b) to account for the discrepancy of the first four lines. Regardless of one's decision on this unresolvable matter, it is clear that no theological motives are present. If the Chronicler's haplography did not in fact take place, he is simply giving the reason for David's sin as being his census of the people by means of a rhetorical question.[5]

Another textual problem has been resolved with evidence from 4QSam[a]. The Chronicles reading, "and I have done very wickedly" (line f), agrees with the 4QSam[a] reading הרעתי. when allowances for the Chronicler's *plene* spelling are made against 2 Samuel's העויתי "I have done perversely."[6] Thus, the Chronicler made no change here in his *Vorlage*.

Rudolph suggests the last clause of the prayer, "but not against your people that they should not be plagued" (line j), is due to "der falschen stellung der Negation . . . und weil man אל erwarten würde, nicht möglich (ist)."[7] He thus suggests we read with Klostermann, וּבָעָם כְּלָא מַגֵּפָה "but against the people restrain the plague." This is an attractive hypothesis, especially since the LXX is reading כלא. The addition may be attributed to simple expansion, completing the thought of the Samuel *Vorlage*. The vocative, "O Yahweh, my God" (line h), may also be seen as simple expansion with no explicit theological motivation.

The other differences arise from the familiar orthographic and linguistic changes we have seen before: the *plene* spelling of "David" (line a), יהוה האלהים (line a), and אני-הוא for הנה אנכי (line e).

---

[3]For a complete discussion see Lemke, "Synoptic Studies," 68ff; and Eugene C. Ulrich, *The Qumran Text of Samuel and Josephus,* (Missoula: Scholars, 1978) 156-157.

[4]NAB, note to 2 Sam 24:17.

[5]For a similar use of rhetorical question in the Chronicler's Royal Prayers cf., 2 Chr 20:6, 7, 12.

[6]For a more detailed argument, see Ulrich, 86-87.

[7]*Chronikbücher,* 146.

4. 2 Chr 1:8-10 = 1 Kgs 3:6-9

	1 Kings	2 Chronicles
a	וַיֹּאמֶר שְׁלֹמֹה	ויאמר שלמה לֵאלֹהִים
b	אַתָּה עָשִׂיתָ	אתה עשית
c	עִם-עַבְדְּךָ דָוִד אָבִי	עִם- דָּוִיד אבי
d	חֶסֶד גָּדוֹל	חסד גדול
e	כַּאֲשֶׁר הָלַךְ לְפָנֶיךָ בֶּאֱמֶת וּבִצְדָקָה	
f	וּבְיִשְׁרַת לֵבָב עִמָּךְ	
g	וַתִּשְׁמָר-לוֹ אֶת-הַחֶסֶד הַגָּדוֹל הַזֶּה	
h	וַתִּתֶּן-לוֹ בֵן יֹשֵׁב עַל-כִּסְאוֹ	
i	כַּיּוֹם הַזֶּה	
j	וְעַתָּה יְהוָה אֱלֹהָי אַתָּה הִמְלַכְתָּ אֶת-עַבְדְּךָ	וְהִמְלַכְתַּנִי
k	תַּחַת דָּוִד אָבִי	תַּחְתָּיו
l	וְאָנֹכִי נַעַר קָטֹן	
m	לֹא אֵדַע צֵאת וָבֹא	
n		עַתָּה יהוה אֱלֹהִים
o		יֵאָמֵן דְּבָרְךָ עִם דָּוִיד אָבִי
p		כִּי אַתָּה הִמְלַכְתַּנִי
q		עַל-
r	וְעַבְדְּךָ בְּתוֹךְ עַמְּךָ	
s	אֲשֶׁר בָּחַרְתָּ עַם-רָב	עַם-רב
t	אֲשֶׁר לֹא-יִמָּנֶה וְלֹא יִסָּפֵר מֵרֹב	
u	וְנָתַתָּ לְעַבְדְּךָ לֵב שֹׁמֵעַ	עַתָּה חָכְמָה וּמַדָּע תֶּן-לִי
v	לִשְׁפֹּט אֶת-עַמְּךָ	וְאֵצְאָה לִפְנֵי הָעָם-הַזֶּה וְאָבוֹאָה
w	לְהָבִין בֵּין-טוֹב לְרָע	
x	כִּי מִי יוּכַל לִשְׁפֹּט	כי מי יִשְׁפֹּט
y	אֶת-עַמְּךָ הַכָּבֵד הַזֶּה	אֶת-עמך הזה הַגָּדוֹל

At first glance, the texts seem to be quite divergent. However, a cataloging of the discrepancies reveals the appropriateness of Curtis's description:

> The passage in Chronicles . . . has been condensed with much
> skill, gaining in force. The somewhat verbose mention of the
> favor shown to David (I K. 3[6]) has been appropriately short-
> ened. The allusion to the son on the throne appears in the
> form of the Messianic promise, a clear suggestion of 2 S. 7,
> which (according to *SBOT*) is later than this narrative in
> Kings. The idea of Solomon's weakness is omitted and the
> phrase "go out and come in" (I K. 3[7]) is happily used to
> express the object of the request for knowledge and wisdom
> that he might go in and out royally before his people.[8]

For the sake of completeness, the familiar orthographic change of the
plene spelling of "David" (line c), the addition of האלהים (line a), and the
condensing of "your servant" (line j, where the Chronicler adds the pronominal suffix ־נִי "me") omitted in line (c), as well as "David, my father"
(line k, where the Chronicler adds the pronominal suffix "him"), should be
noted.

Since these four examples of Royal Prayer have been taken over by the
Chronicler with no significant theological changes, they may be eliminated from those most likely to contain his own distinctive thought. A
different verdict will be reached on the remaining two prayers, which
follow below.

5. 1 Chr 17:16-27 = 2 Sam 17:17-29

The texts of these two long prayers will not be reproduced in their
entirety but only those sections which are of decisive importance.

Rudolph characterizes this section of Chronicles as, "Die Anlehnung an
die Vorlage ist sehr eng; die Differenzen sind nicht grösser . . ."[9] Besides
the usual orthographic and linguistic changes we have seen elsewhere, the
major decisive change is found in v 27 (= 2 Sam 7:29):

	2 Samuel	1 Chronicles
a	וְעַתָּה הוֹאֵל וּבָרֵךְ	ועתה הוֹאַלְתָּ לְבָרֵךְ
	אֶת־בֵּית עַבְדְּךָ	את־בית עבדך
b	לִהְיוֹת לְעוֹלָם לְפָנֶיה	להיות לעולם לפניך

[8]Curtis, 316-317.
[9]*Chronikbücher*, 129.

c	כִּי-אַתָּה אֲדֹנָי יֱהוִֹה דִּבַּרְתָּ	כִּי-אתה יְהוָֹה בֵּרַכְתָּ
d	וּמִבִּרְכָתְךָ יְבֹרַךְ	וּמִבָּרֵךְ
e	בֵית-עַבְדְּךָ לְעוֹלָם	לעולם

By simply changing the Hiphil imperative of יאל in 2 Samuel, הוֹאֵל (line a), to a Hiphil perfect, הוֹאַלְתָּ (line a), the Chronicler has completely transformed the message and function of David's prayer. Where Samuel reads, "you have promised this good thing to your servant; and now *let it please you* to bless the house of your servant . . ." (2 Sam 7:28b-29a); in other words, a petition asking God to fulfill his promise by blessing the house ("temple" or "dynasty"?) of David, the Chronicler's reading ". . . you have promised this good thing to your servant, but now, *it has pleased you* to bless the house of your servant . . ." (1 Chr 17:26b-27a) functions not as petition but rather as praise for fulfilling the promise.

That this is the Chronicler's intention may be seen in certain other alterations in the Prayer:

	2 Sam 7:26b	1 Chr 17:24b
a	וּבֵית עַבְדְּךָ דָוִד	וּבִית- דָּוִיד עבדך
b	יִהְיֶה נָכוֹן לְפָנֶיךָ	נכון לפניך

The Samuel reading, with the imperfect יהיה (line b), "and the house of your servant David *shall be* established before you," is in accord with the future-looking tenor of David's petition in Samuel. By omitting the imperfect יהיה (line b), the Chronicler remains consistent with his view of casting the prayer as praise, "and the house of David, your servant *is* established before you." This reading is also supported by the Vulgate.

	2 Sam 7:29b, c	1 Chr 17:27b, c
a	כִּי-אַתָּה אֲדֹנָי יֱהוִֹה דִּבַּרְתָּ	כִּי-אתה יְהוָֹה בֵּרַכְתָּ
b	וּמִבִּרְכָתְךָ יְבֹרַךְ	וּמִבָּרֵךְ
c	בֵית-עַבְדְּךָ לְעוֹלָם	לעולם

Here again, the different conceptions of David's prayer by the two authors appears. The Samuel text, "For you, my Lord God, have spoken and from your blessing may the house of your servant be blessed forever," or, alternatively, ". . . and from your blessing the house of your servant

will be blessed forever," stresses the future-oriented, petitionary character of the prayer with its use of the Pual imperfect יברך (line b). By using
the Piel perfect ברכת (line a), "you have blessed" instead of דבר, the
Chronicler continues to emphasize the recital of God's past deeds. His
condensation of "from your blessing the house of your servant will be
blessed" (line b) to the Pual participle מברך may be explained as an
attempt to avoid the Pual imperfect יברך. The translation would then be,
"For you, O Lord, have blessed, and it is blessed forever."

The significance of the Chronicler's transformation of this prayer will
become evident in Chapter 5. For the present, it should simply be noticed
that 1 Chr 17:16-27, while it is paralleled in 2 Samuel, has been suffi-
ciently altered to warrant its inclusion among the Chronicler's distinctive
Royal Prayers.

6. 2 Chr 6:14-42 = 1 Kgs 8:23-53

Surprisingly, in light of the Chronicler's propensity, Solomon's long
prayer at the dedication of the temple is remarkably free of alterations in
the two accounts. There are, however, places where the Chronicler has
adapted the prayer to his own conceptions.

1 Kgs 8:25	2 Chr 6:16
לָלֶכֶת לְפָנָי	ללכת בְּתוֹרָתִי

The usual explanation for this alteration of "to walk before me," to "to
walk in my law," deals with the post-exilic emphasis on the law as a way
of life.[10] Thus, the Chronicler is making Solomon's prayer more relevant
to the situation of his community. This may be the reason for his omission
of היום "today" in v 19 where 1 Kgs 8:28b reads ". . . hearken unto the cry
and to the prayer which your servant prays before you *today*." By deleting
the time reference, the prayer becomes applicable to any period in history
especially the Chronicler's own day, and not simply that of Solomon.[11]

The usual orthographic and linguistic modifications seen earlier are
also present with the addition of the Chronicler's curious habit of adding

---

[10]See Frank Michaeli, *Les Livres des Chroniques, d'Esdras et de
Nehemie,* (Neuchatel: Delachaux & Niestlé, 1967) 158; Ackroyd,
Chronicles, 112.

[11]See the discussion of 2 Chr 6:40, below, 60 for another instance.

the particle מִן "from" to every place in Kings that makes reference to where God dwells.[12] This is probably to be explained by the relationship between a God who cannot be held by "heaven and the highest heaven" (2 Chr 6:18) and yet has consented to place his name in the temple so that when prayer is offered toward the temple he would hear and answer (2 Chr 6:18-21).

2 Chr 6:20 displays another tendency of the Chronicler over against his source in that he changes the direct discourse of Yahweh in 1 Kgs 8:29 to indirect discourse. This occurred previously in David's prayer 1 Chr 17:25 = 2 Sam 7:27.

But the major change in Solomon's prayer occurs at the end, just as in the previous example of David's prayer.

	1 Kgs 8:50-53	2 Chr 6:40
a	וְסָלַחְתָּ לְעַמְּךָ אֲשֶׁר חָטְאוּ-לָךְ	
b	וּלְכָל-פִּשְׁעֵיהֶם אֲשֶׁר פָּשְׁעוּ-בָךְ	
c	וּנְתַתָּם לְרַחֲמִים	
d	לִפְנֵי שֹׁבֵיהֶם	
e	וְרִחֲמוּם	
f	כִּי עַמְּךָ וְנַחֲלָתְךָ הֵם	
g	אֲשֶׁר הוֹצֵאתָ מִמִּצְרַיִם	
h	מִתּוֹךְ כּוּר הַבַּרְזֶל	
i	לִהְיוֹת	עַתָּה אֱלֹהַי יִהְיוּ-נָא
j	עֵינֶיךָ פְּתֻחֹת	עֵינֶיךָ כְּתֻחוֹת
k		וְאָזְנֶיךָ קַשֻּׁבוֹת
l		לִתְפִלַּת הַמָּקוֹם הַזֶּה
m	אֶל-תְּחִנַּת עַבְדְּךָ	
n	וְאֶל-תְּחִנַּת עַמְּךָ יִשְׂרָאֵל	
o	לִשְׁמֹעַ אֲלֵיהֶם בְּכֹל קָרְאָם אֵלֶיךָ	
p	כִּי-אַתָּה הִבְדַּלְתָּם לְךָ לְנַחֲלָה	
q	מִכֹּל עַמֵּי הָאָרֶץ	

_____

[12] השמים for מן-השמים (2 Chr 6:21 = 1 Kgs 8:30); אל-השמים for מן-השמים (2 Chr 6:25, 30, 33, 35, 39 = 1 Kgs 8:34, 39, 43, 45, 49); ממכון שבתך for מכון שבתך (2 Chr 6:33 = 1 Kgs 8:43).

r   כַּאֲשֶׁר דִּבַּרְתָּ בְּיַד מֹשֶׁא
            עַבְדֶּךָ
s   בְּהוֹצִיאֲךָ אֶת-אֲבֹתֵינוּ
            מִמִּצְרָיִם
t   אֲדֹנָי יְהֹוִה

As comparison of the two prayers shows, the Chronicler has eliminated virtually all of his *Vorlage*. This is not to say that 1 Kgs 8:50-51 was unimportant to him, however. It will be shown later that he has in fact used this material in another context, namely the crucial speech of Hezekiah in 2 Chr 30:6-9.

In v 40, the Chronicler has used 1 Kgs 8:52 to suggest once again the timeless quality of the prayer. By omitting the reference to "the supplication of your servant" (line m) the Chronicler leaves the time of prayer offered at the temple ambiguous. It will be shown that this prayer of Solomon governs the form and content of all succeeding prayers in Chronicles that are offered by the king and thus, the reason for this omission is to guarantee the timeless nature of the paradigmatic Royal Prayer.

The remaining portions of 1 Kgs 8:51-53 were omitted by the Chronicler because they dealt with the events of the Exodus. North has conveniently summarized the various arguments offered for the Chronicler's lack of interest in this motif.[13] What is of importance here is not only that the Chronicler has omitted these verses but that he has replaced them with material drawn from Ps 132:8-10,1.[14]

Ps 132:8-10,1	2 Chr 6:41-42
	וְעַתָּה
קוּמָה יְהֹוָה	קומה יהוה אֱלֹהִים
לִמְנוּחָתֶיךָ	לְנוּחֶךָ
אַתָּה וַאֲרוֹן עֻזֶּךָ	אתה וארון עזך

---

[13]North, "Theology of the Chronicler," 177-178; also, Ackroyd, "History and Theology," 510-512.

[14]The lack of precise wording has caused some to contest the Chronicler's use of Ps 132. However, Ackroyd argues that, "Since we have numerous examples of psalms which appear in different forms, it is better to suppose that the Chronicler here makes use of a text which has not otherwise survived than to suppose that he has gathered odd fragments together," *Chronicles*, 113.

כהניך יהוה אלהים   כֹּהֲנֶיהָ   וְלִבְשׁוּ-צֶדֶק
ילבשו תשועה
וחסידיך יְשַׂמְּחוּ בַּטוֹב   וַחֲסִידֶיהָ יְרַנֵּנוּ
              בַּעֲבוּר דָּוִד עַבְדְּךָ
יהוה אלהים אל-תשב   אַל-תָּשֵׁב
פני-משיחך   פְּנֵי-מְשִׁיחֶךָ
זכרה   זְכוֹר-יְהוָה
לְחַסְדֵי דָּוִיד עַבְדְּךָ   לְדָוִד אֵת כָּל-עֻנּוֹתוֹ

Williamson has offered the following explanation of this passage: (1) the Chronicler has employed this psalm as the conclusion of his recasting of Solomon's prayer because its main theme is a prayer for David, who has been faithful in his care for the Ark (2 Sam 6), and the recipient of God's promise of an eternal dynasty (2 Sam 7). In the Chronicler's portrayal of David he augments Dtr to show David as assigning a new role to the Levites, a role based upon the superfluous nature of their task as bearers of the Ark (cf. 1 Chr 6:16f; 16:7, 37-42; 23:24-32; 2 Chr 7:6; 8:14f; 35:3), since the temple is now its final resting place (1 Chr 22:19; 28:2). Thus, the Chronicler stresses the fulfillment of this motif in the dedication. (2) Secondly, the Chronicler uses David's last three speeches and concluding prayer to stress the fulfillment of God's promises in the building of the temple (1 Chr 22:7-19; 28:2-10; 29:1-5; 29:10-19). Again, it is not surprising that he mentions this fulfillment in the context of the temple's dedication. (3) The concluding section transforms the function of Solomon's prayer. While the Kings account closes with a request for God to hear the prayers of his people whom he has separated to be his own inheritance, the Chronicler uses the prayer to recall explicitly the fulfillment of God's promise to David through Nathan (1 Chr 17) in the building of the temple.[15] This use, taken in conjunction with the Chronicler's recasting of the prayer as a timeless paradigm, promises God's continual hearing of Israel's prayer as long as it, too, is offered at or toward the temple.

This section has determined six of the Royal Prayers contained in Chronicles are most likely to contain the Chronicler's own distinctive thought: 1 Chr 17:16-27; 29:10-19; 2 Chr 6:41-42; 14:10 (Eng 11); 20:6-12; 30:18f. The next section will provide a more detailed examination of these prayers.

---

[15]Williamson, *Israel*, 64-66.

II.   ANALYSIS OF ROYAL PRAYER

This section will examine those Royal Prayers determined to be from the Chronicler. First, a translation will be offered with notes on the relevant critical details. As in the presentation of Royal Speech, redactional material will be included in brackets. Secondly, the structure of the unit will be presented where the close analogy to the Laments found in the Psalter will be seen. So that the similarity in structural characteristics can be more easily seen, the Royal Prayers unique to Chronicles will be discussed in order of their length, from the shortest to the longest.

1. 2 Chr 14:10 (Eng 14:11)

> Then Asa cried to the Lord his God and said:
>> O Lord, there is none like you to help, between the mighty and the weak:[16]
>> Help us! O Lord our God, for we have relied upon you and in your name we have come against this army.
>> O Lord, you are our God; mortal man cannot[17] prevail[18] against you.

Closer examination of the text uncovers the structure of this brief prayer and shows it to be in the form of a lament.

a	Framework	ויקרא אסא אל־יהוה אלהיו
b		ויאמר
c	Address	יהוה
d	Complaint	אין־עמך
e		לעזר בין רב לאין כח
f	Petition	עזרנו
g		יהוה אלהינו

---

[16]Literally, "there is none like you to help between the great and him with no strength." On the force of עם "beside" or "like" cf. 2 Chr 20:6; Ps 73:25; BDB עם 3d. LXX reads, "it is not impossible for you to save by many or by few," following 1 Sam 14:6, to which LXX[L] has added from the MT, "to him who has no strength."

[17]On אל- + the indicative, cf. Ps 121:3; Jer 46:6 (אל-ינום) and John Gray, The Legacy of Canaan, (Leiden: E. J. Brill, 1957) 203.

[18]כח is understood, (cf. 2 Chr 20:37 and 1 Chr 29:14; 2 Chr 2:5; 13:20; 22:9 where כח follows עצר).

h	Protestation		כי עלך נשענו
i	of Innocence		ובשמך באנו על-ההמון הזה
j	Confession		יהוה
k			אלהינו אתה
l			אל-יעצד עמך אנוש

The prayer falls into four parts (a-b; c-e; f-i; j-l). The first division (a-b) consists of two clauses which provide the introductory framework for the prayer which is explicitly introduced as direct speech by ויאמר. (b). The second division (c-e) is introduced with the vocative, "O Lord" (c) which forms the Address of the lament. This is followed by (d,e) which serves as the Complaint, i.e., "Only you can help against such overwhelming odds," ("one million with the hundred chariots," cf. v 9). The third division (f-i) again is introduced with the vocative, "O Lord our God," (g) in conjunction with the imperative "Help us!" (f). Clearly, this functions as the Petition while the reasons for God's help (h,i) serve as the Protestations of Innocence frequently found in the laments. The fourth, and final, division (j-l) once again is introduced by the vocative, "O Lord," and becomes the Confession of Trust, "You are our God; mortal man cannot prevail against you." These divisions are further evidenced by the change of subject in each: Asa, in (a-b); Yahweh in (c-e); the community in (h-i); and Yahweh again in (j-l). The Assurance is recorded in narrative form in v 11, "Then the Lord vanquished the Ethiopians before Asa and before Judah, so that the Ethiopians fled."

The account of the pursual and חרם which follows in vv 12-14 as well as the reference to the פחד-יהוה displays the Chronicler's adoption of the "Holy War" traditions.[19] His purpose in employing these traditions out of Israel's past is seen in the function of the prayer. By placing the prayer at the beginning of the pericope and using the imperative עזרנו (f), the Chronicler has the prayer call forth the action of God in v 11. As Richter has observed, this is the common function of speeches placed in this position.[20] Thus, the Chronicler uses these traditions to emphasize the powerlessness of man over against God, and the effectiveness of prayer. As Myers says:

---

[19] 2 Chr 15:1ff; 16:7ff; 20:15ff; 32:7ff; etc.

[20] Wolfgang Richter, *Exegese als Literaturewissenschaft: Entwurf einer alttestamentlichen Literaturetheorie und Methodologie* (Göttingen: Vandenhoeck und Ruprecht, 1971) 93.

The victory over Zerah was Yahweh's, a powerful illustration of what could be expected by those who relied upon him. No forces of mortal man can withstand Yahweh.[21]

2. 2 Chr 30:13-22a

13. Many people were assembled at Jerusalem to keep the feast of unleavened bread in the second month—it was a very large assembly. 14. And they arose and removed the altars that were in Jerusalem; they also removed the incense altars[22] and threw them into the Kidron Valley. 15. Then they slaughtered the passover (lambs) on the fourteenth (day) of the second month. Meanwhile, the levitical priests, [being ashamed][23] consecrated themselves and brought burnt offerings to the house of the Lord. 16. As a result, they stood at their place according to their ordinance, as prescribed in the law of Moses, the man of God—now the priests[24] were sprinkling the blood [(which they received) from the hand of the Levites][25] 17. Because many of the assembly had not consecrated themselves [the Levites were in charge of the slaughter of the passover (lambs) for all who were not purified in order to consecrate (them) to the Lord,][26] 18. For many of the people, many from Ephraim, Manasseh, Issachar and Zebulon had not been purified, yet ate the passover

---

[21]Myers, II Chronicles, 85.

[22]LXX and Vulgate explain this *hapax legomena* as "all on which they burnt incense to false (gods)." Curtis thinks the phrase may be a gloss to interpret המזבחות in the previous line as Ahaz's incense altars (cf. 2 Chr 28:4, 25), 474.

[23]MT reads, "the priests and Levites were ashamed and consecrated themselves . . .," but נכלמו "they were ashamed" is lacking in the Syriac which also reads התקדשו for ‐וַיִּתְ and the Vulgate reads *tandem sanctificati,* "being at length sanctified" instead of MT "were ashamed." BH[3] proposes dropping the reference to the Levites as well as נכלמו and reading, "then the priests consecrated themselves," but we read, by dropping the ו on והלוים. והכהנים הלוים with v 27.

[24]וה‐ with many MSS, LXX and Vulgate.

[25]מיד הלוים is deleted with BH[3] as a secondary expansion which not only is quite at odds with the Chronicler's conception of the offering, but also displays "Constructionsänderungen und Unebenheiten im Satzgefüge," see Büchler, 117-119.

[26]Another expansion which adds to the stature of the Levites, see Willi, 200.

without (doing) as it was written. But Hezekiah prayed for them, saying:

> O Lord, make atonement for the good,[27] (that is) 19. everyone who has set his heart to seek the Lord[28] God of his fathers, yet not according to the purifications of the sanctuary.

20. And the Lord listened to Hezekiah and healed the people. 21. The Israelites present in Jerusalem kept the feast of the unleavened bread for seven days with great joy, and praised the Lord day by day [the Levites and the priests with all their might[29] to the Lord. 22a. Then Hezekiah congratulated[30] the Levites, who had shown good skill (in the conduct of the service) of the Lord.][31]

a	Narrative	ויאספו ירושלם עם-רב
b		לעשות את-חג המצות בחדש השני
c		קהל לרב מאד
d		ויקמו ויסרו את-המזבחות אשר בירושלם
e		ואת כל-המקטרות הסירו
f		וישליכו לנחל קדרון
g		וישחטו הפסח בארבעה עשר לחדש השני
h	Narrative	והכהנים הלוים התקדשו

---

[27] The MT reads, "May Yahweh the good pardon . . ." (יהוה הטוב יכפר) בעד:), ending the verse in the middle of the clause. Most translators opt to remove the *soph pasuk*. However, יהוה הטוב has no parallel in Hebrew and the LXX reads κύριος ἀγαθός without the article. In addition, LXX^L (b e$_2$) and the Armenian read ἐξίλασαι the imperative for כפר (cf. the two examples in the LXX at Lev 9:7). Therefore with Barnes, 262, it is probable that the Hebrew division is correct, but that the order of the words is incorrect. By reading יהוה כפר בעד הטוב (Barnes reads יכפר) and letting הטוב בעד govern הטוב, the ambiguity is resolved. For "the good" cf. 2 Chr 19:11. The next clause defines "the good."

[28] The MT adds האלהים before יהוה but this is lacking in the LXX, Vulgate and Syriac.

[29] Literally, "with strong instruments" בכלי עז. By dropping the *yodh*, with most commentators, we reach our translation (cf. 1 Chr 13:8).

[30] Literally, "spoke to the heart of."

[31] By adding 21b-22, the later hand has changed the subject of ומחללים ל- to "the priests and the Levites," providing a basis for Hezekiah's praise of the Levitical competence. That the verses are redactional is also evidenced by the unparalleled order of the words הלוים והכהנים.

i		ויביאו עולות בית יהוה
j		ויעמדו על-עמדם כמשפטם כתורת משה איש האלהים
k		והכהנים זרקים את-הדם
l	Rationale	כי-רבת בקהל אשר לא התקדשו
m		כי מרבית העם רבת מאפראים ומנשה יששכר
		וזבלון לא הטהרו
n		כי אכלו את-הפסח
o		בלא ככתוב
p	Prayer	כי התפלל יחזקיהו עליהם
q		לאמר
r		יהוה
s		כפר בעד הטוב
t		כל-לבבו הכין
u		לדרש יהוה אלהי אבותיו
v		ולא כטהרת הקדש
w	Yahweh's Response	וישמע יהוה אל-יחזקיהו
x		וירפא את-העם
y	People's Response	ויעשו בני-ישראל הנמעים בירושם
		את-חג המצות
z		שבעת ימים בשמחה גדולה ומחללים
		ליהוה יום ביום

As the table shows, this text falls into six parts which are variously related to each other. The first division (a-g) is a narrative as shown by the *waw* consecutives (a,d,d,f,g). The subject throughout is the עם-רב of v 13 (a), and the narrative describes the reforming activities of the congregation in preparation for the great celebration of the unleavened bread. The second division (h-o) consists of two sections. The first (h-k) is marked by the change in subject from עם-רב to הכהנים הלוים and signals the simultaneous action of another group. This section is to be characterized as a narrative as well, again shown by the series of *waw* consecutives (i,j). The purpose of this narrative is to display the activities of the Levitical priests over against those of the people and culminates in the circumstantial clause, "—now the priests were sprinkling the blood," (k). The second section of this second division (i-o), functions as an extended causal clause giving the reasons for the priests' action in line (k) (זרקים את-הדם). This section is again marked by a change in subject, this time from "the priests" to "many of the assembly." The subject is further clarified in (m) as those members of the North who had responded positively to Hezekiah's letter asking them to return (2 Chr 30:6-9). This leads to the explanation of the priests' "sprinkling of the blood" being due to the uncleanness of the Northerners who were forced to travel to Jerusalem for the feast (cf. Num 9:6ff). That the priests' actions were not entirely satisfactory is shown in the third division, Hezekiah's prayer (p-v). While the three clauses introduced by כי in the last section were employed as causal clauses, the כי in (p), since it follows a negative,[32] must be translated in an adversative sense, "but." Thus, Hezekiah's intercessory prayer must be seen over against the activity of the priests on behalf of the Northern celebrants. The structure of the prayer itself conforms to the Chronicler's use. After the introductory framework + לאמר (p,q) the prayer begins with the vocative "O Lord," (r) and continues with the imperative which functions as a petition. The final three lines of the prayer (t-v) serve to define the idiosyncratic הטוב of (s) and give further evidence of the significance of לדרש יהוה for the Chronicler's theological position. Cultic rules and regulations are of secondary importance in the hierarchy of Israel's obligation, of paramount importance is "seeking the Lord." This division is again marked by a subject change, "many of the assembly" to "Hezekiah," as well as being cast in direct speech. The fourth and fifth divisions (w-x, y-z) are both responses. The fourth, the response of Yahweh to the imperative of the petition, consists of two clauses where Yahweh "hears" Hezekiah (w) and "heals" the people (x). As in Asa's prayer, the powerlessness of man (in this case the priests) over against God, and the effectiveness of prayer are once again emphasized. The fifth division (y-z) recounts the response of the people to the healing activity of God. These divisions are also marked by change of subject.

3. 2 Chr 20:5-12

5. Then Jehoshaphat stood in the assembly of Judah and Jerusalem in the house of the Lord before the new court, 6. and he said:
  O Lord, the God of our fathers:
    Surely[33] you are God in the heavens, and you rule all the kingdoms of the nations.

---

[32]For the adversative sense of כי after a negative cf. Ronald J. Williams, *Hebrew Syntax, An Outline,* 2d ed., (Toronto: University of Toronto Press, 1976) # 555. Kropat takes the כי in the sense of כי-אם here (31).

[33]For rhetorical questions taken as expressions of absolute confidence see *GKC* # 150e and cf., Vulgate, v 6.

In your hand is power and might so that no one can stand against you.

7. Surely you are our God.

You drove out the inhabitants of this land from before your people Israel, in order that you might give it to the seed of Abraham, your friend, forever.

8. They have lived in it and built[34] there a sanctuary for your name saying:

9. If evil, sword, flood,[35] pestilence or famine come upon us, we will stand[36] before this house, before you—since your name is in this house—and cry to you because of our distress, in order that you might hear and save.

10. But now, here are the Ammonites, the Moabites and those from Mt. Seir—whom you would not let Israel invade when they came out of the land of Egypt; instead they went around them and did not destroy them—11. here they are, repaying us by coming to drive us out from your[37] possession which you have given us. 12. O our God: Will you not judge them? For we are powerless before this great army that is coming against us and we know not what we should do. But our eyes are upon you.

a	Address	יהוה אלהי אבתינו
b		הלא אתה־הוא אלהים בשמים
c		ואתה מושל בכל ממלכות הגוים
d		ובידך כח וגבורה
e		ואין עמך להתיצב
f	Recitation of Past Favors	הלא אתה אלהינו

---

[34]MT reads "for you" which is omitted by the LXX, Vulgate and Syriac.

[35]MT has שפוט the infinitive of the verb "to judge," in the sense of a governor or administrator, which does not read easily here. Most follow the Vulgate *gladius judicii* "the sword of judgment" by combining שפט with חרב. Rudolph suggests a metathesis of ט and פ may have taken place, yielding ושטף "flood" as the original reading, 258, cf. Ps 32:6.

[36]The cohortative is translated as a future since it is the apodosis of a conditional clause, *GKC* # 108f.

[37]LXX has κληρονομίας ἡμῶν "our inheritance." MT is correct as the Chronicler thinks of the land as Yahweh's (1 Chr 17:14; 28:5; 29:11, 23) and the LXX could easily arise from the MT reading but not vice versa, see Curtis, 407.

g		הורשת את־ישבי הארץ הזאת מלפני עמך ישראל
h		ותתנה לזרע אברהם אהבך לעולם
i	Protestation of Innocence	וישבו בה
j		ויבנו בה מקדש לשמך
k		לאמר
l	Statement of	אם תבוא עלינו רעה חרב שטף ודבר ורעב
m	Trust	נעמדה לפני הבית הזה ולפניך
n		כי שמך בבית הזה
o		ונזעק אליך מצרתנו
p		ותשמע
q		ותושיע
r	Complaint	ועתה הנה בני אמון ומואב והר שעיר
s		אשר לא נתתה לישראל לבוא בהם בבאם מארץ מצרים
t		כי סרו מעליהם
u		ולא אשר הורשתנו
v		והנה־הם גמלים עלינו
w		לבוא לגרשנו מירשתך
x		אשר הורשתנו
y		אלהינו
z	Petition	הלא תטפט־בם
aa		כי אין בנו כח לפני ההמון חרב הזה
bb		הבא עלינו
cc		ואנחנו לא נדע מה־נעשה
dd		כי עליך עינינו

Otto Eissfeldt has characterized the structure of Jehoshaphat's prayer as part of a national lament, accompanied by fasting (v 3) and answered with the divine oracle (vv 15-17). After listing a number of Psalms belonging to this cultic practice, (Pss 44; 60; 74; 79; 83; 89) Eissfeldt displays the constituent parts using Ps 44 as a paradigm:

1. Complaint (vv 10-17, 20, 26)

2. Plea for help (vv 24-25, 27)

3. Recollection of Yahweh's past favors (vv 2-4)

4. Expression of trust (vv 2-4)

5. Protestation of innocence (vv 18-19, 21-22)

6. Assurance that disaster is due to adherence to Yahweh (v 23)[38]

The structural analysis of the prayer shows Eissfeldt to be correct. 2 Chr 20:6-12 falls into four main divisions (a-e; f-q; r-x; y-dd), the first, second and last of which are introduced by vocatives (a, f, y) and are immediately followed by questions beginning with הלא (b, f, z). That the questions in (a-e) (f-q) are similar in function to the English rhetorical question is shown by the confessions that follow them in (d-e) (g-h). For this reason they are translated as expressions of absolute confidence and not as questions. Further indications of the structural breaks at these points are the change in subject: "You," i.e., Yahweh in (a-h); "They," i.e., Israel in (i-q); "the Ammonites . . . ," i.e., the enemies of Israel in (r-x); and "You," i.e., Yahweh, again in (y-dd), as well as the programmatic ועתה (r) "and now" with which the Chronicler introduces the third division.

Within these four main divisions the characteristics of the national lament are clearly present: the recitation of past favors (v 7; f-h); the protestation of innocence (v 8; i-k); the statement of trust (v 9; l-q), interestingly presented as a quotation from those building the temple and strongly recalling the prayer of Solomon at the dedication of the temple in Chapter 6. The complaint (vv 10-11; r-x) and the petition (v 12; y-dd) complete the list.

Petersen has discerned two irregularities in the structure.[39] The first is the switch to the third person in vv 8, 9, the protestation of innocence and statement of trust. Petersen thinks the use of the third person "implies that the present generation had not and was not saying these sorts of things, that is, saying them on their own." Rather, they appropriated the earlier prayer of v 9 liturgically as a theological precipitate of the lament. In this regard it is interesting to recognize the character of v 9 as a "brief summary of the cases in Solomon's dedicatory prayer in which Yahweh would hear the people's cry, cf. 6:28-30."[40]

The second irregularity, as discerned by Petersen, has to do with the "plethora of questions in the introductory section of the lament . . ."[41]

---

[38]Otto Eissfeldt, *The Old Testament. An Introduction,* (New York: Harper and Row, 1965) 112-113.
[39]Petersen, 72ff.
[40]Curtis, 407.
[41]Petersen, 72.

which is unusual. Normally, the ancient deeds of Yahweh are recited as articles of faith, here they are generalized into vague notions of strength (cf. v 6) or phrased as questions. While questions are not foreign to the lament, they usually appear in the petition as does v 12 (z), "Will you not judge them?" Petersen argues that dismissing these questions as rhetorical questions ignores their character, which is to "create a deeper impression on the hearer than would have been obtained by making a direct statement."[42] Thus, we need to pass lightly over the first three questions (v 6 for Petersen, who lets the initial הלא govern the entire verse) in order to focus on the final one, dealing with Yahweh's dispossession of the Canaanites. This question serves as the foil to the subject of the complaint: Yahweh's sin of omission in ridding Israel of those in the land but failing to do the same to those outside the land.

This approach, however, makes the thrust of the prayer deal with Yahweh's failure to provide in the past. While this is true to some extent, as it appears in the complaint, the major theme of the prayer is Israel's lack of strength and dependence upon Yahweh for victory as seen in the reason for the petition of v 12 (aa). Furthermore, the assurance provided by the speech of Jahaziel (vv 15-17) is directed precisely to this feeling of inadequacy on the part of Israel. It has already been noted that this expression of confidence in the strength of God as well as the awareness of human weakness is the characteristic tone of all of the Chronicler's prayers.

This second speech of the chapter from Jahaziel (vv 15-17) is really a part of the national lament contained in the prayer. Begrich was the first to isolate the priestly salvation oracle as the means of understanding the dramatic change in tone that usually concludes the laments. His suggestion was that this positive response represents the answer of God by some cultic official, usually consisting of three parts:

1. The formula, "Fear not"

2. The designation of the party being addressed

3. The assurance that Yahweh has heard[43]

All three parts are contained in the speech. The formula, "Fear not,"

---

[42]Ibid.

[43]J. Begrich, "Das priesterliche Heilsorakel," *ZAW* 52 (1934), 82ff.

appears in vv 15, 17, the parties are addressed as "all Judah and the inhabitants of Jerusalem, and King Jehoshaphat," in v 15, and the people are assured that Yahweh's strength is enough, they need not even fight the battle (v 15-17).

4. 1 Chr 29:10-19

10. Then David blessed the Lord before all the assembly. David said:
> Blessed are you, O Lord, God of Israel our father,[44] forever and ever. 11. Yours, O Lord, is the greatness, the power, the glory, the eminence and the majesty, indeed[45] everything in heaven and on earth; yours, O Lord, is the kingdom and you have exalted yourself as head over all. 12. Both riches and honor come from you; you rule over all; in your hand are power and might; by your hand you magnify and strengthen all. 13. And now, O our God, we are about[46] to thank you and praise your glorious name. 14. But who am I and who are my people, that we should retain strength(?)[47] [to volunteer like this? Rather everything comes from you and we have given you (only) what has come from your hand.] 15. For we are strangers before you, and sojourners as all our fathers were; our days on earth are like a shadow; there is no hope.[48] 16. [O Lord,

---

[44]Reading "Israel" as the patriarch and not as the nation with most commentators on the basis of v 18. Braun translates, "Blessed are you, Yahweh our father, the God of Israel," since he takes 2 Kgs 11 [sic] :48 as the basis of the text, "Significance," 76.

[45]Cf., Kropat, 31; Curtis, 306; and Carl F. Keil, *The Books of Chronicles,* (Edinburgh: T & T Clark, 1872) 299, for this sense of כי which allows retention of the MT. If כי is translated as "for" we must supply לך after כי with Rudolph in BHS. The verse is corrupt in the LXX.

[46]Cf. *GKC* # 116p; Williams, # 214 for the participle expressing the immediate future. Curtis' suggestion that the emphasis is in the continual thanking and praising cannot be maintained because of the time reference, ועתה 306.

[47]Taking נעצר כח as the end of the clause without the idiomatic כזאת and infinitive construct "to be able to . . ." as in 2 Chr 13:20; Daniel 10:8, 16; 11:6. A later hand has expanded the idea into the following clause which recalls the secondary material of 1 Chr 29:1-5.

[48]Rudolph thinks מקוה is ill-suited to the context if translated as "hope" and argues for "security" as the opposite of צל, (192). This has

our God, all this abundance that we have provided in order
to build a house for you for your holy name has come from
your hand because everything is yours. 17. Since I know, O
my God, that you examine the heart and desire uprightness, I, in the uprightness of my heart, have freely offered
all these things; and now, with joy I have watched your
people, who are present here,[49] offering freely to you.]
18. O Lord, God of Abraham, Isaac and Israel our fathers,
preserve this forever as the frame of mind of your
people,[50] and direct their heart toward you. 19. [And give
a whole heart to Solomon my son, that he may keep your
commandments, your testimonies, and your statutes,
([51] in order to build your house (for) which I have
prepared.][52]

a	Framework	ויברך דויד את-יהוה לעיני כל הקהל
b		ויאמר דויד
c	Address	ברוך אתה יהוה אלהי ישראל אבינו
		מעולם ועד-עולם

---

some merit since the theme of hopelessness apart from Yahweh is
characteristic of all the Chronicler's unique prayers as this study has
shown, and as Plöger (47-48) and Braun ("Significance," 77) surmise,
although Braun rejects Rudolph's reasoning.
[49]The article is attached to the finite verb (a Niphal perfect) as a
substitute for the relative. For other examples see *BDB*, 209; *GKC*, #
138i.
[50]Literally, "the frame (intention) of the thoughts of the heart," which
is "almost impossibly verbose, no doubt due to the quotation of the phrase
from Gen 6:5, cf. also 1 Chr 28:9. That one or another of the words might
be a later addition is a distinct possibility, but impossible to prove,"
Braun, "Significance," 78.
[51]לעשות הכל . "to do everything" is very difficult in this position. Braun
thinks the frequent occurrence of לעשות in other chronistic sections with
strong Deuteronomistic colorings (e.g., 1 Chr 22:13) suggests לעשות may
have been a marginal gloss to לשמור taken into the text at the wrong
place, ibid. This would have taken place quite early as LXX[L] adds πάντα
to the major LXX witness.
[52]MT reads, "in order to build the palace (הבירה cf. v 1) which I have
prepared." The translation above reflects in part the LXX which knows
nothing of הבירה, either here or in v 1. Here, the translation is τοῦ οἴκου
σου, and in v 1 of LXX[B], the word, a Persian word occurring only in these
two places with reference to the temple, is omitted.

d	Hymn of	לך יהוה הגדלה והגבורה והתפארת
	Praise	והנצח וההוד
e		כי כל בשמים ובארץ
f		לך יהוה הממלכה
g		והמתנשא לכל לראש
h		והעשר וכבוד מלפניך
i		ואתה מושל בכל
j		ובידך כח וגבורה
k		ובידך לגדל ולחזק לכל
l		ועתה אלהינו
m		מודים אנחנו לך
n		ומהללים לשם תפארתך
o	Complaint	וכי מי אני ומי עמי
p		כי-נעצר כח
q	Protestation of Innocence	כי גרים אנחנו לפניך
r		ותשבים בכל-אבותינו
s		כצל ימינו על-הארץ
t		ואין מקוה
u	Petition	יהוה אלהי אברהם יצחק וישראל
		אבותינו
v		שמרה זאת לעולם ליצר מחשבות
		לבב עמך
w		והכין לבבם אליך

This final prayer of David is by far the most difficult prayer to account for in the books of Chronicles. It displays many of the characteristics found in the Chronicler's other prayers, such as the use of introductory vocatives and ועתה as well as subject changes to demarcate structural divisions. However, there are a number of elements, present in this prayer, which find no correlation in the other chronistic prayers. Since this study contends that these variations are the direct result of a later expansion which was especially active in all of 1 Chr 29, it seems best to devote an entire chapter of the dissertation to a thorough examination of these problems. Thus, a complete discussion of David's final prayer, 1 Chr 29:10-19, will be included in Chapter 5.

III. SUMMARY

This chapter has examined the Chronicler's Royal Prayers, 1 Chr 17:16-27; 29:10-19; 2 Chr 6:14-42; 14:10 (Eng 11), and demonstrated that they share many characteristics with regard to structure and content. In fact, the Royal Prayers are quite similar to the Royal Speeches that were examined in Chapter 2. The longer prayers contain historical retrospects (e.g., 2 Chr 20:7-9). The prayers are composed in prose rather than the poetic renditions of the Psalter and utilize the same connecting particles in the same way to give the text structural cohesiveness. Frequently, the Royal Prayers include rhetorical questions. It could be said that the Chronicler employs the same form for both his Royal Speeches and Royal Prayers. That which differentiates between the two is to whom the utterance is addressed. A human addressee requires a Royal Speech while God requires a Royal Prayer.

With regard to content, the prayers employ portions of the lament or even entire laments to repeatedly make one point: the contrast between the power and might of Yahweh and the weakness and dependence of his people.

4

Theological *Tendenz* in Chronicles

This study has concerned itself with a portion of the non-synoptic material of Chronicles, the Royal Speeches and Prayers, in a conscious attempt to avoid the methodological problems that have beset those interpreters who have based their findings on the material paralleled in Samuel and Kings. This approach rests, in part, upon the findings of Lemke,[1] but the appropriateness of singling out the non-synoptic material as a corpus to be examined is, a priori, just as proper as investigating the parallels. Although the major conclusion of Lemke's dissertation was that a comparison of the synoptic portions of Chronicles reveals much less tendentious alteration of the *Vorlage* than had previously been assumed, he did find forty-nine[2] of 127 deviations examined to be tendentiously motivated. Lemke then proceeded to group these forty-nine deviations into seven classifications of theological motivation:

    1. Theology of Theocracy: seven examples of Israel being ruled by

---

[1]"Synoptic Studies."

[2]There is some confusion here. Lemke states that only thirty-eight instances of tendentiously motivated alterations were admissible (289). When the alterations are grouped under his seven categories of *Tendenz*, however, a count of forty-six appears (242-246). This tally conflicts with the count at the end of the individual chapters which is forty-seven. This discrepancy apparently has arisen by Lemke's oversight of #32 (1 Chr 21:5 = 2 Sam 24:9) in the last chapter, and the apparent tally of forty-nine in the categories is due to his assigning two of the pericopes #96 (2 Chr 23:1-21 = 2 Kgs 11:4-20) and #127 (2 Chr 34:9 = 2 Kgs 22:14) to two different categories.

God through the two channels of the Davidic dynasty and the Jerusalem temple[3]

2. Pan-Israel: twelve examples concerned to stress the essential unity of sacral Israel[4]

3. Anti-Northern Polemic: five examples denouncing the Northern Alliance's rejection of the theocracy[5]

4. Doctrine of Retribution: twelve examples of individual retribution directed both positively and negatively to the kings[6]

5. Idealization of Pious Kings: four examples concerned to present David, Solomon and Hezekiah in a positive light[7]

6. Cultic Concerns: six examples dealing with the elaboration of worship practices, cultic patterns and the temple[8]

7. Levitical Interests: three examples concerned to augment the status of the Levites[9]

I. CRITIQUE OF LEMKE

Before moving on to an examination of the non-synoptic material with an eye to determining if these theological motivations are also present

---

[3] 1 Chr 17:14 = 2 Sam 7:16; 21:26 = 24:25a; 2 Chr 6:39-42 = 1 Kgs 8:50-53; 7:1-3 = 8:54; 7:12b-15 = no parallel; 9:8 = 10:9; 21:7a = 2 Kgs 8:19a.

[4] 1 Chr 11:1a = 2 Sam 5:1a; 11:4 = 5:6a; 13:5 = 6:1; 13:6a = 6:2a; 14:8a = 5:17a; 15:25 = 6:12b; 21:1 = 24:1; 21:2b = 24:2b; 2 Chr 1:2-3a = 1 Kgs 3:4; 11:3 = 12:23; 23:1-21 = 2 Kgs 11:4-20; 34:9 = 22:4.

[5] 2 Chr 10:2-3a = 1 Kgs 12:2-3a, 10; 18:1-3 = 22:1-4; 20:35-37 = 22:49-50; 22:3-5a = 2 Kgs 8:27; 22:7-8 = no parallel.

[6] 2 Chr 15:19 = 1 Kgs 15:16; 16:12 = 15:23b; 20:35-37 = 22:49-50; 21:10b = 2 Kgs 8:22b; 24:2 = 12:3-4; 24:24 = no parallel; 24:25a = 12:21; 25:20 = 14:11a; 25:27 = 14:19; no parallel = 15:4; 28:5 = 16:5; 28:16-21 = 16:7-9.

[7] 1 Chr 17:13 = 2 Sam 7:14-15; 18:2 = 8:2; 2 Chr 2:14 = no parallel; 32 = 2 Kgs 18-19 = Isa 36-37.

[8] 2 Chr 2:3-5 = 1 Kgs no parallel; 2:6, 13 = 7:13-14; 7:6 = no parallel; 8:11 = 9:24; 8:12 = 9:25; 23:1-21 = 2 Kgs 11:4-20.

[9] 1 Chr 15:26 = 2 Sam 6:13; 2 Chr 5:4 = 1 Kgs 8:3; 34:9 = 2 Kgs 22:4.

where the Chronicler is, more or less, freely composing, a brief digression is needed to challenge some of Lemke's findings in the synoptic material. First, four examples that Lemke determines to be motivated by other than tendentious reasons and second, two examples that Lemke attributes to definite *Tendenz* will be examined.

Alterations Motivated by other than Tendentious Reasons in Lemke's Analysis

1. #61 (2 Chr 8:1-2 = 1 Kgs 9:10-23)[10]

In this passage the Kings account states that twenty cities were given *by* Solomon *to* Hiram as remuneration for services rendered. The Chronicler, on the other hand, states that the cities were given *by* Huram *to* Solomon who fortified them and inhabited them with Israelites. Commentators have generally seen this reversal as tendentious, claiming that Solomon obviously had the resources to pay Huram but that the Chronicler's religious sensitivities about Solomon ceding Israel's sacral inheritance to pagans induced him to rewrite history.[11]

Lemke argues against this consensus that (1) the accounts are about the same matter as the Chronicler's placement shows (2) it is incredible that he would have changed the story since he never uses his sources in this way and the readers would surely be aware of his alteration (110). Thus, the Chronicler must have presupposed his readers would have knowledge of the Kings account and merely wanted to add a further comment on the fate of the cities: since Huram refused them, in Kings, it is natural to assume he gave them back to Solomon. While this is possibly historical it is probably an inference on the part of the Chronicler to modify a detrimental picture of Solomon (112).

As to the possible *Tendenz* of the passage, Lemke thinks at best, it evidences a harmonizing exegesis; at worst, a "deliberate and clumsy falsification of history *ad maiorem gloriam Solomonis*" (112f), and chooses the former.

It may be argued, in response to Lemke, that the Chronicler, in his dealings with Huram, is quite concerned to show *Solomon* is in charge of

---

[10]Lemke, "Synoptic Studies," 110-113.

[11]Wellhausen, 187; Kittel, 119; Galling, 97; Rudolph, 219, see the Chronicler using an existing tradition, but his very choice of the tradition over the account in Kings is evidence of *Tendenz,* as Lemke says, "Synoptic Studies," 110.

the building of the temple. In 2 Chr 2:2-9 he omits any mention of Huram's embassy to Solomon (1 Kgs 5:15) to emphasize Solomon's initiative on enacting the commands of David in the speeches of 1 Chr 22-29. Also illustrative of this concern to portray Solomon as in charge of the building of the temple is the Chronicler's editorial handling of 2 Chr 3:15-4:10 = 1 Kgs 7:13-39. In the Kings text, all the third masculine singular pronouns refer to "Hiram." But the Chronicler, by omitting vv 13f of the Kings text and placing the following material after the description of *Solomon's* construction work (2 Chr 3:1-14), makes all the pronouns refer back to Solomon (v 1). Thus, Solomon, and not Huram, is literally the one who "builds" the temple in Chronicles.

In light of this evidence, it seems more appropriate to say the Chronicler had tendentiously altered the Kings text *ad maiorem gloriam Solomonis* at 2 Chr 8:1-2, and assign this text to the category of Idealization of Pious Kings.

2. #115 (2 Chr 28:22-25 = 2 Kgs 16:10-18)[12]

Lemke notices that the passages both speak of the cultic innovations undertaken by Ahaz, but in differing ways: the Kings account describes the innovations while the Chronicler comments on the wickedness of such behavior and adds further measures, especially shutting the temple in vv 24f. Lemke's argument seems to be that it is hard to say if Ahaz's policies took place in *history* since they are not recorded in Kings. Thus he claims the Chronicler's additions are "hyperbolic exaggerations, outgrowths of his utter contempt for Ahaz" (212). But, isn't this precisely what a tendentious alteration is? Williamson has described the reinterpretation of Ahaz in Chronicles as a heightening of "the description of the apostasy of Ahaz"[13] which includes the additions made to Kings in this text, and from the perspective of *Tendenz,* whether or not they actually took place is irrelevant. Thus, 2 Chr 28:22-25 should be viewed as a tendentious alteration of the Chronicler's *Vorlage* although here it is employed to impugn rather than idealize a Judean king.

---

[12]Lemke, "Synoptic Studies," 211-212.
[13]Williamson, *Israel,* 114.

3. #120 (2 Chr 32:24-31 = 2 Kgs 20:1-19)[14]

In describing the sickness and recovery of Hezekiah, Lemke states the Chronicler "goes his own way." He has abbreviated the first eleven verses of the Kings account to one verse (v 24) and added a note (v 31b) which shows "the whole incident was viewed as a temptation sent from God to see whether his (i.e., Hezekiah's) heart was true."[15] The reasons for the abridgment are not clear to Lemke who surmises those dark spots on Hezekiah were not pleasing. But if that is the case, Lemke wonders why the Chronicler retained them, since they are not essential to his picture of Hezekiah and they are not demanded by the context.

In fact, this pericope is quite essential to the Chronicler's picture of Hezekiah. In 2 Kgs 20, the emphasis is strongly placed on the miraculous intervention of Isaiah, the prophet. This is to be expected from the narrative of 2 Kgs 19 where Hezekiah asks Isaiah to intervene on behalf of Jerusalem in the matter of Sennacherib's invasion, and God promises to spare the city in Isaiah's oracle (vv 32-34). In 2 Chr 32:20, however, Hezekiah and Isaiah pray *together* with the result that Sennacherib's forces are routed. This is not to be seen as a diminishing of Isaiah as much as a glorification of Hezekiah which arises out of the Chronicler's conception of prayer and prophecy. In Chronicles it is primarily the king who prays, indeed, this passage is the only reference in which a prophet makes intercession. The prophets, on the other hand, are utilized to preach the doctrine of retributive justice.[16] This same motif is expressed in 2 Chr 32:24 where Hezekiah prays on his own behalf and is answered by the "sign," supposedly recovery. Finally, 2 Kgs 20:12-19 is taken from Isa 39:1ff and is a denunciation of Hezekiah. This denunciation of one of the Chronicler's favorites is taken over in a milder version in 2 Chr 32:25 only to be followed by the pious activities of Hezekiah in verses 26ff and the rationale for Hezekiah's "pride" offered in v 31b.

Thus, when the immediate context of those verses is closely examined, it becomes clear that the Chronicler has tendentiously reworked his *Vorlage* in an attempt to idealize the pious king, Hezekiah.[17]

---

[14]Lemke, "Synoptic Studies," 216.
[15]Ibid., parenthesis added.
[16]See Appendix.
[17]For a similar reconstruction see Newsome, "Prophecy," 39-42.

4. Concluding subscripts to a king's reign

In his last chapter, Lemke has grouped all the occurrences of alleged *Tendenz* that deal with the concluding subscripts of a king's reign or his burial notice in a single category and judges them to be inadmissible for determining theological motivation.[18] With regard to the burial notices, Lemke observes that while the Chronicler's summaries frequently include information that is additional to Kings (e.g., the king was not buried in the royal tomb: 2 Chr 21:20; 22:9; 24:25b; 28:27 or was greatly honored at his burial: 2 Chr 16:13f; 32:33), the judgment of many scholars that the Chronicler has added this material to mark the king as pious or godless is not confirmed by the evidence, since this suggested principle of interpretation is not consistently applied. Many times the Chronicler follows his *Vorlage* closely, adding nothing,[19] and since the additional information is reasonable, it is not to be questioned.

Lemke deals with the citation of sources in these subscripts in a similar way. The contention of many scholars, that the Chronicler has "freely invented" this material due to the frequent citation of sources not found in Kings, is no indication of *Tendenz* since there is no uniformity in the sources mentioned and since the text is in a state of flux, it is possibly due to later editors. Lemke does agree that one cannot disprove *Tendenz* in these examples, one can only caution against the problems in maintaining such a view.[20]

Hans Engler has arrived at the opposite conclusion with what he terms "the Deuteronomistic Verdict."[21] Engler compares the instances of the Deuteronomistic Verdict in Kings and Chronicles in a variety of ways and concludes that while it is relatively easy to present a survey of the Judean kings congruent with the three categories the DtrH has distinguished [i.e.,

---

[18] 2 Chr 9:29 = 1 Kgs 11:41; 12:15-16 = 14:29-31; 13:22 = 15:7; 16:11 = 15:23a; 16:13-14 = 15:24; 20:34 = 22:46; 21:20 = 2 Kgs 8:23-24a; 22:9 = 9:27-28; 24:25b = 12:22b; 24:27a = 12:20; 25:26 = 14:18; 26:22 = 15:6; 26:23 = 15:17; 27:7 = 15:36; 28:26 = 16:19; 28:27 = 16:20; 32:32 = 20:20; 32:33 = 20:21; 33:18-19 = 21:17; 33:20 = 21:18. 2 Chr 25:27 = 2 Kgs 14:19, also listed in this category is tendentious due to the retributionism in the passage, Lemke, "Synoptic Studies," 233.

[19] E.g., 2 Chr 9:29; 12:5-6; 13:22; 20:34; 33:20; ibid., 234.

[20] Ibid, 234-235.

[21] "The Attitude of the Chronicler Toward the Davidic Monarchy," (Th.D. dissertation, Union Theological Seminary in Virginia, 1967), especially 1-13.

(1) those kings that did that which was "right" (2) those that did that which was "evil" and (3) those that did that which was "right" in their personal conduct, but did not remove the high places where the people were worshipping], it is not easy to do so with the Chronicler.[22] In marked opposition to the DtrH, who

> allowed his judgment upon any one king to be dominated by the respective king's attitude toward idolatry, the Chronicler judges a king, first of all, by his personal conduct, further, not only by his attitude toward idolatry but also by his concern over the worship of the true God, and last not least, by his obedience to the Word of God, as contained in the "Law" of Moses or proclaimed by the prophets; even the kind of burial given to a king seems to reflect a judgment on his conduct in life.[23]

Engler's work shows that the Chronicler was very consistent in his application of the Deuteronomistic Verdict and that where he agrees with Kings it is simply a matter of having the same opinion as his predecessor, although sometimes for different reasons. Furthermore, Engler has demonstrated that the Chronicler is using the subscripts with much more freedom and for a different purpose than the author of Kings. Thus, Lemke has perhaps been too zealous in his explusion of this material from the Chronicler's observable *Tendenz*.

Alterations Motivated by <u>Tendenz</u> in Lemke's Analysis

1. #59 (2 Chr 7:6, no parallel)

This passage is obviously based upon the content of 2 Chr 5:11b-13a which is a later addition to the Chronicler's work.[24] Thus, while it is definitely tendentious, it does not arise from the Chronicler and cannot be used to characterize his theology.

---

[22]Ibid., 11.

[23]Ibid., 12.

[24]On the redactional character of this verse see Rudolph, 217; and Willi, 196.

2. #65 (2 Chr 8:11 = 1 Kgs 9:24)

This study has determined that the portion of 2 Chr 8:11 that differs from the Kings *Vorlage* is redactional.[25] Thus, it too must be left out of consideration for determining the Chronicler's theology.

Interestingly, this examination has argued that in these cases the *Tendenz* of the Idealization of Pious Kings is more pronounced than Lemke claims. This is curious since the idealization of pious kings is all but absent in the non-synoptic material. Obviously, this kind of statistical analysis must be used with great caution as the results of such investigation in the synoptic portions of the Chronicler's work appear to conflict with those arrived at from the non-synoptic portions.

II. COMPARISON OF NON-SYNOPTIC TENDENZ

This study has investigated a sizable portion of the non-synoptic portions of Chronicles. When the Royal Speeches and Prayers are examined for Lemke's seven theological motivations, the following collations appear:

1. Theology of Theocracy
   a. Speeches: 1 Chr 22:1, 10; 28:5 (if chronistic); 2 Chr 13:5-8 all lend positive support
   b. Prayers: No evidence
2. Pan-Israel
   a. Speeches: 1 Chr 13:2; 28:4, 8 (if chronistic); 2 Chr 19:8; 30:6; 34:21 all lend positive support
   b. Prayers: 2 Chr 30:18 lends positive support
3. Anti-Northern Polemic
   a. Speeches: 1 Chr 13:2, 2 Chr 30:6-9 provide negative evidence
   b. Prayers: 2 Chr 30:18 provides negative evidence[26]

---

[25]See 29f.

[26]While the instances cited in this collation as providing positive support from the Royal Speeches and Prayers are self-evident, brief discussion of those providing negative evidence is in order. In 1 Chr 13:2, David makes it clear that his concern is for all Israelites, especially those "brothers" who are in all the land of Israel. 2 Chr 30:6-9, as we have seen, is Hezekiah's summons to the North to return, his concern is again typified in his calling the Northeners "brothers" (v 9). This is confirmed in

4. Retribution
    a. Speeches: 1 Chr 15:13; 22:13; 28:7, 8, 9 (if chronistic); 2 Chr 13:12; 14:6; 20:20; 28:23; 29:8, 9, 10; 30:7, 9, 9 all lend positive support
    b. Prayers: No evidence
5. Idealization of Pious Kings
    a. Speeches: 1 Chr 22:8 provides negative evidence[27]
    b. Prayers: No evidence
6. Cultic Concerns
    a. Speeches: 1 Chr 15:12; 22:1, 5; 2 Chr 13:9, 10; 29:5, 6, 7, 10, 11 all lend positive support. 1 Chr 22:14; 28:26; 29:1-5; 2 Chr 8:11 lend positive support if they are chronistic
    b. Prayers: 2 Chr 30:19 provides negative evidence[28]
7. Levitical Interests
    a. Speeches: 1 Chr 28:21 and 2 Chr 29:5 support Levites as Arkbearers. 1 Chr 15:2; 23:26; 2 Chr 13:9, 10, 11; 19:8, 9, 11 only lend positive support if they are chronistic
    b. Prayers: No evidence

As the collations show, Lemke's determination of the Theology of Theocracy, Pan-Israel and Retributionism as theological concerns of the Chronicler is strongly supported by this non-synoptic material. However, his categories of Anti-Northern Polemic and Idealization of Pious Kings are contradicted by these findings. Furthermore, the categories of Cultic Concerns and Levitical Interests are inconclusive. From the speeches that are certainly chronistic, the Levites are only depicted as bearers of the Ark, and the Cultic Concerns deal primarily with the Ark and later, David's general provisions for the temple. This is not surprising for four reasons:

---

his prayer (2 Chr 30:18) where Hezekiah prays for those Northerners who heeded his earlier summons.

[27] 1 Chr 22:8 can hardly be spoken of as idealizing David since, in contrast to 1 Kgs 5:3, the reason for God's forbidding David to build the temple is moral in that David "has shed much blood." In Kings, the reason is expediency, David was too busy fighting.

[28] 2 Chr 30:19, in which Hezekiah flouts the cultic prescriptions for participation in the cult by saying that all that is needed is to have "set one's heart to seek God," cannot be adduced to support a rigid legalism in cultic matters.

1. These last four categories have the lowest numerical support of Lemke's seven categories.

2. The concern for "All Israel" is clearly at odds with an Anti-Northern Polemic

3. Lemke states (245) that the way the Chronicler usually idealizes pious kings is to *omit* derogatory material, but, by definition, the non-synoptic portions cannot be examined in this way

4. The Cultic and Levitical Concerns derive, in large measure, from a later hand and are thus not indicative of the Chronicler's theology

In a more positive vein, two examples of theological concern not identified by Lemke have emerged:

1. Theology of "Rest"

Roddy L. Braun has done the most extensive work in this area.[29] In 1 Kgs 5:17-19 (Eng 5:3-5), David's failure to build the temple is regarded as a consequence of his not having sufficient time, due to the fact that he was engaged in warfare. The Chronicler, however, has reinterpreted this passage in 1 Chr 22:7-13 to show that David's wars and the bloodshed that resulted disqualified David, "the man of war" (1 Chr 28:3), from undertaking the project which was given to Solomon, the "man of peace" to whom Yahweh will give "rest" from his enemies.

Building upon the earlier studies of G. von Rad[30] and R. A. Carlson,[31] Braun examines the importance of the concept of "rest" for Deuteronomy and the deuteronomistic history, stating that while the usages of the term cluster around three important events, the conquest of the land by Joshua

---

[29]See Braun, "Solomon, the Chosen Temple Builder," 581-90, especially 582-586 and note 13.

[30]"There Remains Still a Rest for the People of God: An Investigation of a Biblical Conception," in *The Problem of the Hexateuch and other essays,* trans. E. W. Trueman Dicken (Edinburgh: Oliver & Boyd, 1966) 94-102.

[31]R. A. Carlson, *David, the Chosen King* (Stockholm: Almqvist & Wiksell, 1964) 97-106.

(Josh 1:13, 15; 21:44; 22:4; 23:1), the dynastic promise to David (2 Sam 7:1, 11), and the building of the temple by Solomon (1 Kgs 5:18; 8:56),

> the singular importance of *menuha* for our study is most apparent from Deuteronomy 12, where the unification of the cult is specifically related to Israel's rest in the promised land (583).

For the Chronicler, the idea of a God-given rest in the promised land, in that it marked the fulfillment of the promises to Israel, was the necessary prerequisite for the building of the temple, and was enjoyed by Solomon, the chosen temple builder in a way not experienced by David.

This theology of rest is most clearly exhibited in the Royal Speeches. 1 Chr 22:8, 9, 18; 28:2; 2 Chr 14:6 have all been influenced in some way by this concept. Further support for seeing David's speech in 1 Chr 23:25ff as stemming from a later hand arises from v 25, where the redactor has not appreciated this concept of rest in Chronicles. The redactor writes:

> For David said, "The Lord, the God of Israel has given rest (RSV: peace) to his people; and he dwells in Jerusalem forever."

With regard to tendentious changes, the Chronicler, in taking over 2 Sam 7:1 at 1 Chr 17:1, has omitted the clause:

> now the Lord had given him (i.e., David) rest from all his enemies round about,

from his description of the Nathan Oracle.[32] Also, in 2 Chr 15:19 = 1 Kgs 15:16 (#79 in Lemke's arrangement), the Chronicler rewrites the Kings Text:

> Now there was war between Asa and Baasha king of Israel all their days,

to read

---

[32]Lemke does not deal with this crucial text in his study which is by no means comprehensive.

Now there was *no* war until the thirty-fifth year of the reign
of Asa,

as a direct consequence of this concept of rest as well as Lemke's determination of a retribution *Tendenz*.

2. Help from Yahweh Alone

This study has uncovered a second theological motivation that is frequently found in the Chronicler. The concept of help from Yahweh alone,
which often contrasts the omnipotence of God with the dependence of his
people is the major concern of the Royal Prayers occurring at 1 Chr
17:16; 29:15; 2 Chr 14:10; 20:6, 12.[33] In the Royal Speeches it is to be
found at 2 Chr 2:5f; 13:12; 32:7, 8.

III. SUMMARY

In light of the above, Lemke's work is in need of some revision. Most
seriously, a study that is more comprehensive than Lemke's is needed
before scholarship can pass any certain judgments upon the presence of
Tendenz in the Chronicler's work. However, these criticisms of Lemke are
not intended to diminish the real value of his work: the uncovering of
thirty-one examples of textual difficulties, either in Chronicles or the
Vorlage, that have previously been assumed to be indicative of the Chronicler's theological stance. This evidence alone is sufficient to call into
question any method which assumes the Chronicler was utilizing a *Vorlage*
basically similar to our Massoretic Samuel/Kings, and which draws theological conclusions on the basis of an uncritical comparison of the two,
without also checking the evidence provided by the LXX and Qumran.

---

[33]See Chapter 3, 63, 67, 71, 75.

5

1 Chr 29: Royal Speech,
Royal Prayer, Redaction

The purpose of this chapter is two-fold: first, to apply what was discovered in the analysis of Royal Speech and Royal Prayer to a recent attempt to find redactional material in 1 Chr 29; and second, to see if the results of that application can be of assistance in determining the date at which the Chronicler wrote. 1 Chr 29, then, will serve as a test case for the applicability of the results of Part One. Since it contains a Royal Speech (vv 1-5), a Royal Prayer (vv 10-19), redactional, structural and theological difficulties in the first twenty-five verses, 1 Chr 29 is ideally suited for this role.

I. THE UNITY OF 1 CHR 29

Rudolph Mosis is the only scholar to challenge the unity of 1 Chr 29:1-19.[1] His reasons for doing so are as follows:

1. In vv 1, 19, the word chosen to refer to the temple, בירה is very unusual,[2] and the context gives no reason as to why the same author, who has always designated the temple with בית or משכן should now use this Persian loan word. Another unusual word for the temple, בית הקדש occurs in v 3 again, unique to this portion of Chronicles.

2. The whole address comes too late. David has already presented Solomon to the assembly as his successor and builder of the temple in

---

[1] *Untersuchungen zur Theologie des chronistischen Geschichtswerkes* (Freiburg: Herder, 1972) 105-107.

[2] Only here in Chronicles with reference to the temple. Other occurrences in the Old Testament are: Esth 1:2, 5; 2:3, 5, 5, 8; 3:15; 8:14; 9:6, 11, 11; 9:12; Dan 8:2; Neh 1:1; 2:8; 7:2, 2; all with reference to the palace of the Persian king in Susa.

1 Chr 28:2-12a. Moreover, he has installed Solomon as king and encouraged him to proceed with his work in 1 Chr 28:20f.

3. David's programmatic speech concerning his own preparations for the temple, necessary because of Solomon's youth and inexperience, was reported in 1 Chr 22:2-5. Mention of these preparations is much more appropriate before Solomon's installation. In fact, with regard to content, 1 Chr 29:1-9 repeats what has already been said in 1 Chr 22:2-11 and 28:2-7a, 21.[3]

4. The proportions of materials employed by David for the preparations, listed in 1 Chr 22:2-5, have been greatly exaggerated in 1 Chr 22:14-19, recognized as a later addition by all who see secondary expansion in Chronicles. The same exaggeration is found in 1 Chr 29:4. In neither instance do the figures or the cost of the materials stand in any relation to the quantities given in 2 Chr 3ff, the report of the temple construction. Neither do we find reference to the precious stones mentioned in 1 Chr 29:2b.

Furthermore, the verb used to describe the overlaying of the walls with gold and silver in 1 Chr 29:4 is טוח, which only occurs here in Chronicles. In the actual report of the temple construction, 2 Chr 3ff, the usual words for metal-plating are used.[4]

5. In v 19, David asks Yahweh to give Solomon a "whole heart" (לבב שלם), that he might keep the commandments and consequently carry out all that was needed for the construction of the temple. This keeping of the commandments is referred to here, and in 1 Chr 22:12f, 28:7b, 9f, as a condition for the success of the project. Mosis rejects all these references as secondary since they contradict the unconditional nature of the Chronicler's Nathan Oracle in 1 Chr 17 = 2 Sam 7.[5]

6. In the following pericope, 1 Chr 29:20-25, there is a tension which is most easily resolved by being seen as a consequence of the insertion of 29:1-19. The time reference למחרת היום ההוא "on the next day" (v 21) separates the object, עלות ליהוה, "burnt offerings to Yahweh" from its

---

[3](1) the choice of Solomon (29:1b cf. 28:5b); (2) the greatness of the task and Solomon's weakness (29:1b cf. 22:5a); (3) David's preparations (29:2-5a cf. 22:2-5); (4) the people's cooperation (29:6-9 cf. 28:21).

[4]צפה (Piel): 2 Chr 3:4, 6, 10; 4:9; 9:17 and חפה (Piel): 2 Chr 3:5, 5, 8, 9.

[5]This argument is not convincing. See H. G. M. Williamson, "Eschatology in Chronicles," *Tyndale Bulletin* 28 (1979) 138-139 for a critique and ibid., 140ff for a discussion of the intrinsic nature of the conditional aspects of Solomon's response to the Chronicler's overall presentation.

proper apposition, פרים אף- "a thousand bulls, etc." Also, it is not apparent why the time reference is picked up again in v 22 and emphasized in the ביום ההוא "on *that* day."

The simplest explanation would be that the notice in v 21 became necessary after the presentation of Solomon in chap 28 was separated from the people's acknowledgment in 29:20ff by the intrusion of the great contributions of vv 1-19. Since the gathering of gifts took time, the presentation of the offering and Solomon's anointing became difficult to accommodate on the same day. Therefore, the awkward, "on the next day, (after) this day" was inserted to make the festival appear as if it lasted for two days. Removal of vv 1-19, as well as the time reference in v 21, restores the original sense of the emphasis "on *that* day" in v 22, that is, immediately and without delay, even on that day of presentation, the assembly responds to the presentation of Solomon by anointing him and recognizing his kingship.[6] Thus, in the Chronicler's conception, the sacrifice celebration, in which Solomon was anointed, immediately followed David's presentation of the future king in 28:21.

7. With the removal of 1 Chr 29:1-19, as well as 1 Chr 22:12-16 and 1 Chr 28:7b-18,[7] and all of chap 23-27, the structural unit 1 Chr 22-29 receives a clear and lucid sequence:

a) Since David had undertaken many preparations for the temple construction because Solomon was unequal to the task due to his youth and inexperience (1 Chr 22:2-5), he transferred the building of the temple to Solomon in a testamentary address (1 Chr 22:6-13).

b) In order to establish Solomon as his successor, David then called a convention, presented Solomon as his successor and future builder of the temple (1 Chr 28:1-12a) and encouraged him to begin work (1 Chr 28:20f).

c) David's invitation to praise and worship (1 Chr 29:20) introduces the great sacrifice, meal and celebration in which Solomon is anointed.

---

[6]It should be noted that this emphasis on the people's immediate acceptance harmonizes well with the invariable universality of appeal that Solomon enjoys throughout Chronicles.

[7]Most would only agree on the redactional nature of 22:14-16 and 28:12b-18. See note 5, above.

d) All Israel immediately acknowledges Solomon's kingship (1 Chr
29:20-25) and the chapter concludes with a brief summary of
David's reign (1 Chr 29:26-30).

Mosis' reconstruction provides a convenient starting point for an examination of the applicability of the analysis of Royal Speech and Royal
Prayer. It will be shown that Mosis' arguments regarding David's speech
(vv 1-5) can be supported while his conclusions regarding David's prayer
(vv 10-19) must be considerably modified.

Royal Speech and 1 Chr 29:1-5

In Chapter 2, it was discovered that the Chronicler's Royal Speeches
can be classified in three categories: edict, rationale or oration. The
edicts and orations are characterized by their use of imperatives (or their
equivalents in the case of some of the orations) to introduce the major
concern of the speech. In addition, the longer orations frequently contain
historical retrospects relating events of the past to the present situation.
Finally, the logical progression of the speeches is regularly marked with
connecting particles such as עתה, הנה, כי.

When David's speech in 1 Chr 29:1-5 is compared with this general
overview of Royal Speech in Chronicles, several inconsistencies appear:

1. While vv 1-2 are in the form of an historical retrospect, they do not
recall events of the past as much as they relate to the present situation.
As Braun remarks, "verse 3 moves almost imperceptibly into the
present."[8]

2. While the speech retains a hortatory tone and calls Israel to contrib-
ute for the temple, the exhortation is not introduced until the end of the
speech in v 5b. Furthermore, instead of being introduced by an imperative, the imperative has become a pleading question: "Who then is willing
to consecrate himself this day to Yahweh?" (v 5b).[9]

3. We have come to expect connecting particles in the Chronicler's
speeches to mark the logical progression of the speech. In 1 Chr 29:1-5
the progression is artlessly marked with "and" in vv 2, 3, 5b.

4. The usual introductory formula for David's speeches is: ויאמר דויד
ל- plus the addressees (1 Chr 13:2; 22:7; 28:20; 29:20) or ויאמר דויד

---

[8]"Significance," 72.

[9]Braun also recognized this discrepancy but stops short of assigning the
speech to a later redactor, ibid., 72-73.

(1 Chr 22:1, 5). The usual pattern for the other kings is: ויאמר ל- plus the addressees (1 Chr 15:12; 2 Chr 14:6; 19:6; 35:3). In no case is the subject of אמר, דויד המלך, as it is here, in v 1.

These comparisons with the corpus of Royal Speech strongly support Mosis' contention that 1 Chr 29:1-5 is of a secondary nature. Since vv 6-9 form the people's response to the speech, they, too, must be seen as later expansion.

Royal Prayer and I Chr 29:10-19

In Chapter 3, it was discovered that the Royal Prayers are quite similar to the Royal Speeches in Chronicles. The longer prayers contain historical retrospects (e.g., 2 Chr 20:7-9). The prayers are composed in prose rather than the poetic renditions of the Psalter. They are replete with the same connecting particles that function in the same way and frequently include rhetorical questions.

With regard to content, the prayers employ portions of the lament or entire laments to repeatedly make one point: the contrast between Yahweh's power and might and the weakness and dependence of his people.

As it now stands, David's prayer (1 Chr 29:10-19) does not easily fit in the above description. That its character and tone have been altered through subsequent additions will be apparent after a closer examination.

David's final prayer consists of an introductory narrative framework (v 10a,bα) and three main divisions (vv 10bβ-12; 13-17; 18-19), each of which opens with a highly stylized liturgical formula containing some form of the vocative (a structuring device of the Chronicler as is his use of ועתה in v 13). As in the Chronicler's other prayers, these divisions are also marked by a change of subject: "you" i.e., Yahweh (vv 10b-12), "we" i.e., David and the assembly (vv 13-17) and "you" i.e., Yahweh (vv 18-19).

There is wide-spread agreement that these three divisions uncover the structure of the prayer. Discussion arises, however, as to what kind of prayer this is. Myers and Rudolph describe it as a "thanksgiving" emphasizing vv 13-17.[10] Michaeli and Goettsberger, emphasizing vv 10-12, prefer the description "hymn of praise."[11] Braun, who recognizes the prayer as being different from the other chronistic prayers, suggests the Chronicler has ignored distinctions in prayer types and combined three forms together: a hymn of praise in vv 10-12, evidenced by the introduc-

---

[10]Myers, *I Chronicles*, 197; Rudolph, 191.

[11]Michaeli, 140; Goettsberger, 197.

tory blessing of Yahweh and the extended description of his attributes; a thanksgiving in vv 13-17, recognized by the statement of v 13, "Now we thank you," as well as the relationship between v 14 and the prior contributions; and petitions in vv 18 and 19, as shown by the three imperatives, "preserve," "direct" and "give."[12]

It has been shown that a second hand is responsible for 1 Chr 29:1-9. Mosis thinks the same hand is responsible for 1 Chr 29:10-19, but his only evidence is the appearance of בירה in verse 19 and the conditional treatment of the Nathan Oracle in David's petition for Solomon, also in v 19. This study has agreed with Mosis on the secondary character of vv 1-9, but cannot do so with regard to vv 10-19. However, this is not to say that a second hand has not been present. Vv 14b, 16-17 and 19 are products of the redactor since they refer back to the secondary material of vv 1-9. Vv 10-14a, 15 and 18 remain as the original creation of the Chronicler. When this secondary material is removed, the tone of the prayer is altered in the following ways:

1. Vv 10-12 remain as a hymn of praise in which the omnipotence of God is recalled in terminology drawn from the Psalter. Significantly, the introductory formula of blessing is addressed to Yahweh in the second person, ברוך אתה, "Blessed are *you*." While this convention is normal in post-biblical contexts, this and Ps 119:12 comprise the only occurrences in the Old Testament. In earlier contexts, the benediction spoke of Yahweh in the third person and functioned as proclamation to the congregation before the prayer was offered, as W. Sibley Towner has shown.[13] By addressing the benediction to אתה יהוה "you, O Lord," the Chronicler has brought this initial section of the prayer into conformity with the last section, which contains the petition. This third section, like the first, offers no difficulties since v 18 is clearly a petition made on behalf of the people with reference to the middle section (vv 13-14a, 15).

2. It is this middle section that has suffered most in the transmission of the text as well as being the most difficult to classify. However, when the later accretions are removed, the classification becomes obvious. It reads as follows:

> 13. And now, O our God, we are about to thank you and praise your glorious name.

---

[12]Braun, "Significance," 72-73.

[13]"'Blessed be YHWH' and 'Blessed Art Thou, YHWH': The Modulation of a Biblical Formula," *CBQ* 30 (1968) 391ff.

14a. But, who am I and who are my people that we should retain strength?

15. For we are strangers before you, and sojourners as all our fathers were; our days on the earth are like a shadow; there is no hope.

Clearly, v 14a is a complaint in the form of a rhetorical question, strongly set off from v 13 by the use of the double adversative וכי which is unique to this place in the entire Old Testament.[14] The Chronicler's propensity for such rhetorical questions has already been noted.[15] Here, it functions as a counterpoint to the praise and thanksgiving the people are about to offer.

In the midst of God's grandeur and glory, the description of which has practically depleted Hebrew vocabulary, the Chronicler constructs a lament in v 15 based upon the words of Pss 39:12 and 90:5. The people are depicted as powerless and transient, entirely dependent upon God, as were their fathers. A comparison with the Chronicler's other prayers shows this feeling of God's omnipotence over against his people's dependence to be a major theme:

1 Chr 17:16   Who am I, O Lord God, and what is my house that you have brought me thus far?

2 Chr 14:10   Lord, there is no one besides you to help between the powerful and those who have no strength; so help us, O Lord our God, for we trust in you, and in your name have come against this great army. O Lord, you are our God; let not mortal man retain strength against you.

2 Chr 20:6   Power and might are in your hand, so that no one can stand against you . . .

---

[14]But see Ehrlich, where he reminds us that it occurs in the Babylonian Talmud as an introduction to rhetorical questions, 352.

[15]Cf. the prayer of Jehoshaphat (2 Chr 20:6-12) where rhetorical questions appear five times (vv 6, 6, 7, 7, 12); and David's other prayer (1 Chr 17:16-27) where they appear four times (vv 16, 16, 18, 21).

2 Chr 20:12   . . . we are powerless before this great army
                 that is coming against us; nor do we know
                 what to do; but our eyes are upon you.

It is to this recognition of dependence that the אזת, the "this," and the plea of v 18, "and direct their hearts to you," refer.

Seen in this way, David's final prayer is thoroughly consistent with the form and content of the Chronicler's other Royal Prayers and should be retained in a discussion of the Chronicler's structure and theology.

II. 1 CHRONICLES 29 AND THE DATE OF THE CHRONICLER

In the following chapter of this study, it will be shown that the primary argument for dating the books of Chronicles no earlier than 420 B.C. is the presence of the Persian loan words "darics" (v 7) and "palace" (vv 1, 19) in 1 Chr 29. The conclusions of this chapter, however, reveal that these words are contained in that material that appears to be of a later origin. Thus, the presence of "darics" and "palace" in 1 Chr 29 would seem to argue for an earlier dating of the Chronicler's basic work and a subsequent redaction of that material around 400 B.C.[16]

---

[16]For more detail, see Chapter 6, below.

6

Dating the Chronicler

No other book in the Old Testament has been the recipient of more conjectured dates than Chronicles. A partial listing of these dates with their respective supporters will illustrate the range of scholarly opinion in this regard:

515	Freedman, Cross, Newsome, Porter, Petersen
420	Young, Elmslie
400	Albright, Rothstein-Hänel, van Selms, Eissfeldt, Myers
390	Rudolph
360	Bowman, Bentzen
350	Ackroyd
325	Gelin, Kuhl
310	Robert
300	Benzinger, Curtis-Madsen, Galling, Kittel, DeVaux, Welten
280	Noordtzij, Haller
250	Pfeiffer, Torrey, Goettsberger, Noth, Cazelles
165	Lods, Bousett, Kennett

The key to understanding the variety of these dates lies in recognizing a prior commitment on the part of these scholars to the extent of the Chronicler's work.

If the Chronicler's work includes the Ezra-Nehemiah material, one needs to date Chronicles no earlier than 420 B.C. Also, one needs to take into account Greek references to Nehemiah. The lists of high priests in Neh 12:10f, 22f go up to Jaddua whom Josephus reports as high priest in the time of Alexander the Great (333). Furthermore, Neh 12:22 refers to Darius as "the Persian" an explanation which implies the fall of the

98 Royal Speech and Royal Prayer in Chronicles

Persian Empire. Consequently, those scholars who accept Ezra-Nehemiah as part of the Chronicler's work tend to date him around 300 B.C.

If the Chronicler's work contains the genealogies of 1 Chr 1-9 one needs to deal with 1 Chr 3:19-24 where the descendants of Zerubbabel are listed. Unfortunately, the MT and the LXX disagree here, with the MT giving six generations after Zerubbabel while the Greek, Syriac and Vulgate give eleven. If one allows a generous thirty years per generation, the date of Anani (v 24) would be about 350 B.C. Allowing a more realistic twenty-five years per generation, the date would come to about 400 B.C. based upon the MT. If the eleven generation scheme of the LXX is followed, one would arrive at 250 B.C., thus the popularity of these three dates. The evidence, however, is further complicated by the probability that due to scribal error the MT may only list four or even two generations after Zerubbabel rather than six.

If one can speak of a consensus in this matter, it would have to be 400 B.C. with further evidence given by the mention of darics in 1 Chr 29:7 which, according to numismatic evidence, cannot be earlier than the time of Darius (521-486).

Recently, this consensus of opinion has been strongly challenged by a variety of scholars[1] who have based their work upon the findings of D. N. Freedman[2] who sees the Chronicler's work, best situated in the post-exilic restoration of the temple under Zerubbabel and Joshua the high priest, as an historical expression of the movement associated with Haggai and Zech 1-8. Thus, these scholars argue for a date of 520-515 B.C.

H. G. M. Williamson has provided the most cogent arguments against this early dating.[3] Williamson offers three main objections:

1. 1 Chr 3:19-21 carries a genealogy two generations past Zerubbabel and so argues against the early dating.[4] Proponents of the 520-515 dating invariably argue that 1 Chr 1-9 is not part of the Chronicler's work, usually in a circular fashion, since it conflicts with their dating. But, there is at least some problem with attributing this material to the Chronicler as the commentaries show. Williamson himself acknowledges:

---

[1]Cross, "A Reconstruction"; Newsome, "New Understanding"; Porter, "Old Testament Historiography"; Petersen, *Late Israelite Prophecy.*
[2]Freedman, "Purpose."
[3]Williamson, "Eschatology," 120ff.
[4]The textual difficulties of 1 Chr 3:21b-24 are acknowledged by Williamson but are not relevant to his purpose, ibid., 21.

> It could never be proved of course, that a later editor has not
> added a few generations to the Davidic genealogy in order to
> bring it down to his own day . . . (122).

It seems safest, therefore, to reserve judgment on this evidence until the
other indications of dating can be examined.

2. There is a reference to "darics" in 1 Chr 29:7. Williamson collects
the increasingly convincing amount of evidence[5] showing that "Darius I
was the first to mint darics, and that only some years after his accession"
(123) and concludes that:

> Since no one has suggested relegating this passage to a secon-
> dary level of composition it appears that he could not then
> have written as early as Freedman, Cross and Newsome have
> suggested. With that conclusion, however, their understanding
> of the Chronicler's purpose as somehow intending to support
> the hopes vested in Zerubbabel in the early years of Darius'
> reign and as attested in Haggai and Zech 1-8 must be rejected
> (126).

But, Mosis, whose work Williamson cites (132ff), has questioned the
authorship of 1 Chr 29:1-19[6] and this study, while modifying his results
somewhat with respect to David's Royal Prayer in 1 Chr 29:10-19[7] has
added additional arguments for seeing 2 Chr 29:1, 9 as redactional. If
these arguments are convincing, the appearance of "darics" as well as
"palace" in 1 Chr 29:1, 19 would argue for dating this *revision* of the
Chronicler's work somewhere in the reign of Darius (521-486 B.C.). Obviously, the Chronicler's material has to pre-date the revision of that material and one would suppose that the arguments of Freedman, Cross,
Newsome and others, that the "cluster of concerns"[8] for kingdom,
prophecy and cult that converge in the time of Haggai and Zech 1-8 and
which are prominent in Chronicles, best explain the evidence.

3. There are difficulties in seeing a link between Chronicles and
Haggai, Zech 1-8. Williamson points to the different understanding of the
role of Zerubbabel in the two prophets that most recent comparative
studies of Haggai and Zech 1-8 find (126ff). Especially telling is the

---

[5]Ibid., 123-126.
[6]Mosis, *Untersuchungen*, 105-106.
[7]See Chapter V, above.
[8]Newsome, 215.

elevation of the role of Joshua the high priest in Zechariah to the point that it is necessary to speak of a "dyarchic form of leadership in the community."[9]

Although Ackroyd[10] is reluctant to establish precise correlations between history and the dates in Haggai and Zech 1-8, he attached great significance to Zech 1-7 (February, 520 B.C.) since it is quite appropriate to the following passage 1:8-17 which speaks of all the earth remaining at rest. Williamson thinks this is at odds with those scholars who find in Zerubbabel an insurrectionist who was subsequently removed for his rebellious attitude, especially since there is evidence to refute this: (1) Ezra 6:6-7 reports that Darius explicitly confirmed Zerubbabel as governor and (2) Ezra 4 claims "the adversaries of Judah and Benjamin" waited until the reign of Artaxerxes to accuse themselves of being "rebellious and wicked." Thus, Williamson concludes:

> Zerubbabel himself preferred not to make any capital whatever out of his Davidic ancestry (128).

At once, we must interject that Zerubbabel making capital of his Davidic ancestry is beside the point. The question is, did Haggai, Zechariah and the Chronicler do so? Williamson deals with this by stating that if the prophets and the Chronicler cherished such a hope focused upon the house of David in the person of Zerubbabel as Newsome supposes (214), then the evidence suggests that these hopes were modified within months of their formulation. And that:

> Since part of that modification is to introduce the high priest in a role and status which, as Beuken has shown, could not have claimed support from Chronicles, we are left, on Newsome's understanding, with far too short a time to allow for the composition of so long and well structured a work as 1 and 2 Chronicles . . .[11]

But Beuken's analysis[12] is not convincing. After claiming:

---

[9]Williamson, "Eschatology," 127.

[10]P. R. Ackroyd, "Two Old Testament Historical Problems of the Early Persian Period," *JNES* 17 (1958) 13-27, quoted in Williamson, ibid.

[11]Williamson, "Eschatology," 128-129.

[12]W. A. M. Beuken, *Haggai-Sacharja 1-8: Studien zur Überlieferungsgeschichte der frühnachexilischen Prophetie,* Studia Semitica Nederlandica 10 (Assen: Van Gorcum, 1967) 309-316.

> Dass es auch einige Punkte gibt, in denen die Joshuaüberlie-
> ferung von der Thematik und der Terminologie, wie wir sie im
> chronistischen   Geschichtswerk   vorfinden,   abzuweichen
> scheint (309).

Beuken first notices the differences in terminology for the High Priest in
Haggai-Zech 1-8 (הכהן הגדול) and the Chronicler (כהן הראש). There is a
difference here, but that the Chronicler was not opposed to such terminology is shown by his use of הכהן הגדול unchanged from his *Vorlage*
(2 Kgs 22:4) at 2 Chr 34:9. Furthermore, the simple כהן is used frequently
in Chronicles, and shows the Chronicler employing a variety of terms for
the office.

Secondly, Beuken observes that theological reflection on the High
Priest is not present in the Chronicler's work which merely reports the
High Priest's presence (311ff). But there are at least five passages that
describe the activity of the High Priest,[13] although it must be admitted
that these are scanty and open to discussion.

Thirdly, Beuken discusses three passages in which the Chronicler has
altered his *Vorlage* to show that "Das Königtum hat für den Chronisten
keine kultische Funktion" (314):

1. In 2 Sam 6:14 David wears an אפוד בד, the vestiture of the High
Priest as Exod 28:4ff shows. In taking over this passage the Chronicler has
David wear a מעיל בוץ in 1 Chr 15:27. However, Beuken fails to see that
in the same verse David is described as wearing the אפוד בד in addition to
the מעיל בוץ and there are no real arguments for seeing this as a later
gloss. Furthermore, the Chronicler either misreads the Samuel מכרכר
"danced" as מכרבל "was clothed" and thus completed v 15a with מעיל
בוץ, the Levitical garment, since David, too, was bringing up the Ark, or
he intentionally altered מכרכר not to suppress David's priestly function but
to augment it as only priests can wear the מעיל בוץ.[14]

2. In 2 Sam 6:13, 17 David is described as sacrificing an ox and a fatling
as well as offering whole burnt offerings and peace offerings. In adopting
this passage the Chronicler has allegedly substituted a plural subject to
avoid mentioning David as offering sacrifice and thus functioning as priest

---

[13] 1 Chr 16:39-40; 2 Chr 19:11; 2 Chr 23; 2 Chr 26:16ff; 2 Chr 34:8-28.

[14] Van Selms sees the Chronicler making use of the old tradition of
David as priest-king, "Men zeit, hoe David hier naar oud-Jeruzalemsche
traditie als priesterkonig optreedt," quoted in Lemke, "Synoptic Studies,"
38.

in 1 Chr 15:26; 16:1. But Engler says, "in the context, the only subject is 'David' and no other subject explaining the sudden plural of the predicate is here introduced."[15] Furthermore, the 4QSam[a] materials agree with the Chronicler in this verse against the MT of Samuel[16] in a number of ways. Unfortunately, the relevant word זבח is obscured, but the damaged condition of the Samuel text argues against placing too much confidence in its witness.

Engler has collected further evidence that shows David did function as High Priest.[17] In at least seven places where there is no possibility of confusing the actions of David with the priests, David is given priestly functions:

a.	זבח	Qal:	1 Chr 15:26 which alters 2 Sam 6:13
			1 Chr 21:28 = 2 Sam 24:24f
b.	עלה	Hiphil:	1 Chr 16:2 = 2 Sam 6:18
			1 Chr 21:24 = 2 Sam 24:24
			1 Chr 21:26a = 2 Sam 24:25a
c.	קרב	Hiphil:	1 Chr 16:1 (the parallel 2 Sam 24:25a has עלה Hiphil)
d.	ברך בשם-יהוה	Piel:	1 Chr 16:2 = 2 Sam 6:18

Thus, it is incorrect to state that David, at least, did not participate in priestly functions.

3. In contrast to 2 Sam 8:18b which states: "David's sons were priests," 1 Chr 18:17 says they were "chief about the king." After presenting the evidence, cited above, Engler states in reference to this verse:

> If the Chronicler, indeed, presented David as "priest," his statement that the sons of David were "chief about the king" cannot be considered substantially different from his source . . .[18]

Lemke would appear to agree, although in this one instance he gives no verdict on *Tendenz*, since he noted the variety of interpretations given to

---

[15]Engler, 64.
[16]See Ulrich, *Qumran Text*, 136, 148, 159, 177, 182, 196, 206, 210.
[17]Engler, 40ff.
[18]Ibid., 42.

כהן in the versions.[19] It will be shown below that if our interpretation of 1 Chr 29:22 is correct, there was no longer any need for the king to function as priest in the manner of David.

Closely associated with this linking of Haggai-Zechariah is the question of the redactional history of Haggai-Zechariah and Chronicles. Here, Williamson criticizes Beuken's main conclusion that Haggai-Zech 1-8 received their final editing in a "Chronistically orientated milieu." He notices that this:

> Implies a certain distinction between the original oracles of the prophets and their editors who intended to interpret and reapply their message to a later generation, a distinction which forms the main basis for Beuken's detailed exposition" (130).

Hans Engler has shown that the Chronicler's view of the structure of the theocracy is most closely paralleled by the structure envisioned in Zech 1-8.[20] He examines 1 Chr 29:22 as the clearest indication of the Chronicler's conception and finds that Solomon is anointed נגיד and Zadok is anointed כהן by David, who thus institutes the theocracy. Further examination of נגיד in Chronicles reveals that the king functions as נגיד על עמי ישראל (1 Chr 11:2 = 2 Sam 5:2; 1 Chr 17:7 = 2 Sam 7:8; 2 Chr 6:5b = 1 Kgs 8:16 where the Kings parallel has dropped out by homoioteleuton), and the priest as נגיד בית האלהים (2 Chr 31:13; 35:8). This distinction in function is less clearly seen in 2 Chr 19:11 where the דבר המלך are overseen by a commissioner of the king and the דבר יהוה are overseen by the priest. Thus, Engler writes concerning the structure of the theocracy:

> God's reign over his people is manifest in two offices, that of the Davidic king and that of the Zadokite high priest. The high priest is responsible for matters pertaining to the temple inaccessible to the king, all other matters are the king's responsibility.
>
> This "structure of the theocracy," represented by two anointed ones, king and high priest, may be interpreted as the logical result of the king, contrary to historical fact, being

---

[19]Lemke, "Synoptic Studies," 52-56.
[20]Engler, 44ff.

considered a layman and therefore, having no access to the temple's most holy place; consequently, the leadership over the true "Israel" could not be held by the king alone, as the only anointed one in accord with historical fact, but there was needed a complement for the temple's most holy place. This "complement," the other anointed one, then came to be the high priest (49).

Engler has clearly shown the Chronicler's conception of the structure of the theocracy to be dyarchic. After examining examples of other dyarchic structures in the centuries following the Chronicler[21] he states:

This survey suffices to demonstrate that the Chronicler's conception of a (past, present or future) theocracy repre- sented by king and high priest, comes nearest to that of the prophet Zechariah (59).

This is confirmed by the striking similarity of the two structures:[22]

a. Solomon and Zadok stand side by side and both are anointed 1 Chr 29:22 (cf. Zech 4:3, 11, 14)
b. Solomon sits on God's throne 1 Chr 29:23a (cf. Zech 6:13 the only other instance of God's throne being occupied by a man)
c. God bestows הוד on Solomon (cf. Zech 6:13 where the recipient is איש צמח i.e., Zerubbabel)
d. David founds the temple alone, without the high priest (cf. Zerubbabel in Zech 4:6-7, 8-10; 6:13; Hag 2:20-3)

The differences in the structures which Engler finds are all present in Ezra and Nehemiah, not in Chronicles (55f). If we are arguing for a 520-515 B.C. date for Chronicles, this material is obviously not revelant.

As Williamson acknowledges[23] there are other, general similarities between these prophets and Chronicles. Newsome discusses (1) retributive justice in Zech 1:4ff; Hag 1:9ff; 2:10-14 (2) concern for the temple in Zech 1:7-17; Hag 1:9ff; 2:10-14 (3) messianic hopes focused upon David's house in Hag 2:20-3 (cf. Jer 22:24 which applies the "signet ring" to a

---

[21]E.g., The Testaments of the Twelve Patriarchs; The Manual of Discipline; the "Serek ha-'eda," etc.

[22]Engler, 54-55.

[23]Williamson, "Eschatology," 129-130.

Davidide); Zech 6:12ff. (4) the omnipresence of Yahweh in Zech 1:10; 4:10; 6:1 (cf. 2 Chr 19:6) (5) Judah's seventy year punishment in Zech 1:12; 7:5 (cf. 2 Chr 36:21) (6) the centrality of Jerusalem in Zech 1:16f; 2:1ff; 2:12; 3:1ff; 8:1ff; 8:14f (7) the attribution of evil to Satan/the satan in Zech 3:1 (with the article, cf. 1 Chr 21:1 without the article).[24]

Recent studies on the redaction of Zech 1-8 help to confirm these views and offer assistance in the dating of the material. In a brief article,[25] L. Sinclair has summarized the present research and offered a description of the stages of transmission in Zech 1-8. He uncovers four groups of material. Group one consists of the original visions of Zechariah which share a number of similar characteristics.[26] Sinclair claims:

> The meaning of the passages of this group is that the Lord has plans to restore Jerusalem and that he is about to put his plans into effect. The major emphasis in these verses is the promise of renewal and restoration. Galling suggests that these visions date to the exilic period. Also, there is no major emphasis on the rebuilding of the temple; just 1:16 "my house shall be built in it (Jerusalem)." If Cross is correct in his suggestion that Zechariah came to Jerusalem with Zerubbabel about 520 B.C., in [sic] this material could have originated in Babylon and used as words of encouragement to the people to return to Jerusalem with Zerubbabel (39).

Sinclair thinks the material which originated in Babylon can be more closely dated to 527 B.C. since 1:12 mentions the seventy years of exile (i.e. 597-527 B.C.), and:

> If all the earth is at rest (1:13), [sic] this would fit the conditions of the time. 527 is just before Cambyses began his march toward Egypt and the defeat of Psammetichus in 525 B.C.[27]

---

[24]Newsome, "Prophecy," 184ff.

[25]L. A. Sinclair, "Redaction of Zechariah 1-8" *Biblical Research* 20 (1975) 36-47.

[26]Zech 1:7-17; 2:1-4 (Eng 1:18-21); 2:5-9 (Eng 2:1-5); 4:1-6a, 10b-14; 5:5-11; 6:1-8; 8:1-3; ibid., 38.

[27]Ibid., 40.

Group two consists of expansions to the visions made when the group was in Palestine, again, bearing similar characteristics.[28]

Group three contains material which has close affinities with the prose sections of Jeremiah and Ezekiel, and shares common elements.[29] The references in this material (the 5th, 10th, 7th and 4th months) refer to the seventy year period since the destruction of the temple, not just the destruction of Jerusalem.[30] Thus, since this agrees with the situation in the fourth year of Darius, the material can be dated to 518-517 B.C.

Group four, the material added by the final redactor and which highlights Joshua the High Priest, is contained in Zech 3:1-7; 3:8; 3:9; 3:10 and the addition of "Israel" in 2:2 (Eng 1:19) and "and house of Israel" in 8:13.[31] Sinclair claims this material:

> Gives an eschatological meaning to the whole book. The passages that were used to urge people to hope in the restoration of Jerusalem are changed to have eschatological significance.[32]

The dating of this final redaction needs to be interpreted in this light. The problem with suggesting that the change of "Zerubbabel" to "Joshua" in 6:9-14 arose after the completion of the temple due to the weakness of Zerubbabel is that it is an argument from silence, due to the paucity of historical information. However, Sinclair argues that the substitution of "Joshua" in 6:11 took place after the death of Zerubbabel because:

> the redactor who wanted Joshua to have an important position in the community was seeking to supply a legitimate substitute for the Davidic line which had died out; also, to establish an indigenous ruler in Judah, other than the Persian appointed governor. The redaction of Zechariah would give support to the High Priest's claim (47).

In Cross's theory of the three editions of the Chronicler's work it is

---

[28]Zech 2:6-13; 4:6b-10a; 6:9-14, 15; 7:4-7; 8:9-13; ibid., 40ff.

[29]Zech 1:2-6; 5:1-4; 7:1-3; 7:8-10; 7:11-14; 8:4-8; 8:14-17; 8:18-19; 8:20-23; ibid., 42ff.

[30]For the evidence from Kings and Jeremiah see ibid., 44, n. 61.

[31]Ibid., 45ff.

[32]Ibid., 46. For a similar approach see B. A. Childs, *Introduction to the Old Testament as Scripture* (Phladelphia: Fortress Press, 1979) 476ff.

possible to see the same movement. Chr[1] supported Zerubbabel, while Chr[2] and Chr[3] change to support the hierocracy.[33] Thus we must see this final redaction of Zech 1-8 occurring at 450-400 B.C.

Looking back at the points of similarity between Zechariah and Chronicles we see that they all occur before this final redaction (if Zerubbabel is restored to the text in Zech 6:11). Since these can be dated from 527-517 B.C. there is ample time for the Chronicler to construct his work. As a result, we are compelled to date the basic work of the books of Chronicles in this period.

---

[33]Cross, "A Reconstruction," 16.

7

The Chronicler's
Periodization of History

A recent trend in the study of Chronicles is to examine the Chronicler's structuring of the monarchy, the narrative portions of the books of Chronicles, with an eye to uncovering his basic message. After summarizing Noth's seminal work and briefly examining three of these attempts to reveal the Chronicler's structural framework, this chapter will try to synthesize their results and augment the reconstruction with insights gleaned from the study of the Royal Speeches and Prayers.

I. RECENT APPROACHES

Martin Noth's *Überlieferungsgeschichtliche Studien*[1] is the most comprehensive study of the Old Testament usage of speeches and prayers. In the first part of his examination, Noth analyzes the Deuteronomistic History and proposes that the author made extensive use of speeches, prayers and summaries, composed by the author and placed on the lips of key people at decisive points in the narrative, to clarify the course of events and draw the practical consequences of human actions. These speeches offer invaluable insight into the theology of the DtrH and provide the basis for Noth's structuring of the history in five major periods. With certain revisions, mostly dealing with authorship and dating, Noth's proposal has become a working hypothesis of subsequent Old Testament scholarship.

It is surprising, then, that when Noth turns to an analysis of the Chronicler's history in the second part of his examination, he arrives at an altogether different picture of the Chronicler's usage of speeches. Noth claims that while the Chronicler has composed the speeches and prayers

---

[1]Halle: Max Niemeyer Verlag, 1943.

and inserted them into his narrative, he has not done so at decisive points in the narrative that might reveal his structural framework.[2]

Otto Plöger

Otto Plöger, in an older article that has only recently received the attention it merits, has challenged Noth at this point.[3] For Plöger, the speeches in Chronicles serve to (1) lift up important sections such as the time of David and Solomon and the building of the temple, (2) to demarcate broad periods of time such as the period of the Divided Monarchy, and (3) to emphasize high points in the narrative, especially by using detailed prayers.[4]

Two insights in particular have a direct bearing upon the concerns of this chapter. First, Plöger observes that the speeches of Abijah (2 Chr 13:4-12) and Hezekiah (2 Chr 30:6-9) share a common intention as *"Umkehrreden"* ("calls to return") addressed to the Northern Kingdom.[5] As such, they set off the period of history between them as a time of two churches. Second, Plöger proposes that the time of David and the time of Solomon, usually seen as two distinct periods, are in reality to be understood as a unity with David's preparations for and Solomon's construction of the temple forming "einen zusammenhängenden Akt."[6] Furthermore, the prayer David utters at the coronation of Solomon (1 Chr 29:10-19), since it mirrors David's earlier prayer (1 Chr 17:16-27, taken over from DtrH) serves to enclose David's preparations for the temple.[7]

Roddy L. Braun

The major conclusion of Roddy L. Braun's dissertation[8] serves to substantiate Plöger's contention that the period of David and Solomon is to be understood as a unity. The David History (1 Chr 10-21) and the Solomon History (2 Chr 1-9) are usually seen as separate units. The material in between (1 Chr 22-29, with the omission of 1 Chr 23-27 which is redactional) is usually understood as part of the David History since David's

---

[2]Ibid., 5, 156, 160-161.
[3]Plöger, "Reden und Gebete."
[4]Ibid., 60.
[5]Ibid., 57-58.
[6]Ibid., 56.
[7]Ibid., 57.
[8]Braun, "Significance."

death is not recorded until 1 Chr 29:26-30. But this material is equally concerned with Solomon as he is the center of attention and is anointed in 1 Chr 29:22b-25 prior to David's death. As Braun succinctly puts it:

> Since we have reason to believe that the Chronicler has constructed these two portions of his history as a single unit which has its exact center neither in David nor Solomon, but in the temple and its cult, it seems best to label the unit as transitional.[9]

Furthermore, Braun has attempted to balance the distorted picture of the reigns by stating:

> The Chronicler has obviously designed his narrative to present two kings of equal standing before Yahweh and Israel and of equal devotion to the cult. Neither is exalted or denigrated at the expense of the other, but the reigns of both are presented according to the same general framework.[10]

Three items in particular substantiate Braun's claim that David and Solomon are treated comparably: (1) Both are selected by divine choice (1 Chr 17:11; 22:7-10); the only instance of בחור being applied to a king other than David is with reference to Solomon in 1 Chr 28:6. (2) Both ascended to the throne with the full support of "all Israel" (1 Chr 29:22b-25a). (3) Both were equally devoted to the temple cult.[11]

H. G. M. Williamson

Where Braun's work has substantiated Plöger's observation of the unity of the reigns of David and Solomon, H. G. M. Williamson has indirectly offered evidence in support of Plöger's observation that the speeches of Abijah (2 Chr 13:4-12) and Hezekiah (2 Chr 30:6-9) form a parenthesis around the period of the Divided Monarchy.[12]

Williamson's point of departure is an attempt to answer the question of the status of the Northern Kingdom. As Williamson puts it:

---

[9]Ibid., 11-12.
[10]"Solomonic Apologetic in Chronicles," *JBL* 92 (1973) 511.
[11]Ibid., 507-508.
[12]*Israel*, 110-118.

> That Judah's faithfulness in Chr. by and large to the founda-
> tional traditions of Israel justifies her claim to that name (i.e.
> "Israel") is too well known to need elaboration. But was the
> state of rebellion of the North not so great as to disqualify
> her altogether, as so many commentators have held?[13]

Williamson argues this was clearly not the case at the point of division. Two *Vorlage* retentions claim that the division was due to God, that his word might be established (2 Chr 10:15; 11:4); also, the prophet Shemiah refuses to let Judah coerce the North into union while retaining the title "brothers" for the North (2 Chr 11:1-4). Thus, Williamson agrees with Welch that at the point of division, the Chronicler thought, "there were good reasons for Israel having refused to endure the rule of the Judean king."[14]

But at the point of Abijah's speech (2 Chr 13:4-12), the situation has been reversed. While Rehoboam was king, the North would not have been helped by association with Judah because of his evil character. Rehoboam: (1) "Forsook the law of Yahweh" (12:1), (2) "trespassed against Yahweh" (12:2), (3) "forsook him" (12:5) and (4) "did that which was evil because he set not his heart to seek Yahweh" (12:14). Because of the Chronicler's doctrine of immediate retribution, however, Abijah begins with a clean sheet, and while Abijah is a "bad king" in Dtr, he is a "good king" in Chronicles. Now, the North would surely be helped by association with Judah and her pious king, Abijah, and so, the Chronicler constructs a summons to return and places it on the lips of the king.

This interpretation of Abijah's speech is at odds with the scholarly consensus, which sees the speech as an Anti-Samaritan Polemic. But Williamson points out that (1) the legitimacy of the Davidic Dynasty was irrelevant in the post-exilic situation, (2) the mention of "sons of Aaron" is favorable to the North and (3) the major point of tension, the locality of the chosen sanctuary, is never referred to.[15] Thus, the character of Abijah's speech reveals it to be a summons to the North, inviting them to return, as Williamson states:

> Indeed, Abijah's speech itself should not be understood only in
> terms of negative polemic, but be seen to contain in its
> delicate handling of the division and interpretation of the

---

[13]Ibid., 110 (parenthesis added).
[14]*Post-Exilic Judaism*, 189, quoted in Williamson, *Israel*, 111.
[15]Williamson, ibid., 112.

Northerner's apostasy as "forsaking" God an appeal for just such an act of repentance.[16]

The Northerners' refusal is seen as indicative of their rebellion, and their subsequent defeat is Yahweh's judgment upon them (v 18). That they remain with this status in the remainder of the narrative can be seen from the Chronicler's omission of every Northern historical event which does not have some correlation with Judah.

By altering the Ahaz material of 2 Chr 28 the Chronicler provides a solution to this problem. According to the Chronicler, Judah, under Ahaz, was guilty of the same rebellion as Israel under Jeroboam, as the similar vocabulary shows, and thus, at the time of Hezekiah, *both* kingdoms stood under Yahweh's judgment.[17] The achievement of Hezekiah was the reunification of the separate states.[18]

II. THE STRUCTURAL SIGNIFICANCE OF THE ROYAL SPEECHES

In Chapter 2 it was shown that the Royal Speeches, at least, do tend to be situated at decisive points in the narrative. Further examination of the speeches will reveal a tripartite structuring of the Chronicler's narrative with Plöger's identification of the parenthesis formed by the speeches of Abijah and Hezekiah comprising the basic structural element:

I. The United Monarchy
    A. David: 1 Chr 13:2a, 3; 15:2, 12f; 22:1, 5, 7-13, 18f; 28:2f, 6f, 9f; 29:20
    B. Solomon: 2 Chr 2:3-10; 6:2-11 (= 1 Kgs 18:12-21)
II. The Divided Monarchy
    A. Abijah: 2 Chr 13:4-13
    B. Asa: 2 Chr 14:6
    C. Jehoshaphat: 2 Chr 19:6f, 9-11; 20:20
    D. Ahaz: 2 Chr 28:23
    E. Hezekiah: 2 Chr 29:5-11; 30:6-9

---

[16]Ibid., 114.
[17]Ibid., 114ff.
[18]Ibid., 125.

III.   The Re-united Monarchy
    A. Hezekiah: 2 Chr 32:7-8
    B. Josiah: 2 Chr 35:3a, 5b-6

Period One: The United Monarchy

Plöger,[19] Braun[20] and Williamson[21] are all agreed that the Chronicler
is concerned:

> to present the reign of David and Solomon as a single, unified
> event within the divine economy for the life of the nation, in
> which the complementary nature of the two kings' functions
> plays an important role . . .[22]

When the Royal Speeches of this period are examined as to their content,
the aptness of this description is revealed. In the Davidic speeches the
theme of David's preparation for the building of the temple constituted
the main point:

1. 1 Chr 13:2f; 15:2 (if chronistic), 12ff deal with David's procure-
   ment of the Ark
2. 1 Chr 22:5, 14; 28:2 explicitly state David's preparations for the
   temple
3. 1 Chr 22:3-10, 20f state that David cannot build the temple
   because he has shed blood, but that Solomon, whose name means
   "peace," has been chosen to complete the building for which
   David has prepared
4. 1 Chr 22:1 is a rationale for David's preparations, establishing
   Ornan's threshing floor as the site of the temple

In the Solomonic speeches the theme of Solomon's completion of the
task initiated and prepared for by David, the building of the temple,
constitutes the main point:

---

[19]"Reden und Gebete," 56-57.

[20]See "Apologetic," 503-16; idem, "Solomon the Chosen Temple
Builder: The Significance of 1 Chronicles 22, 28, and 29 for the Theology
of Chronicles," *JBL* 95 (1976) 581-590; idem, "The Message of Chronicles:
Rally Round the Temple," *CTM* 22 (1971) 502-514.

[21]"Eschatology in Chronicles," 132, 140-141.

[22]Ibid., 140.

1. 2 Chr 6:7-9 repeats the promise made to David through Nathan and adds that now the promise has been fulfilled in Solomon (v 10)
2. 2 Chr 2:3-10 is the beginning of Solomon's activity for the building of the temple

Additional evidence for this interpretation is found in the speech made by Yahweh in this section, which is paralleled in the earlier account. In 2 Chr 1:8-12 = 1 Kgs 3:4-14 and 7:12-22 = 9:3-9 Yahweh addresses Solomon as in Kings, but the intention of the Deuteronomistic text, to separate the reign of Solomon into a positive and a negative period, has been suppressed.[23] The Chronicler thus strengthens his conception of the ideal period he has presented in the combined reigns of David/Solomon, Period One.

Plöger also makes mention of the frequent *"Ermunterungsreden"* ("speeches of encouragement") which David addresses to Solomon (1 Chr 22:7-16; 28:9-10, 20f) and the assembly (1 Chr 22:18f; 28:2-8; 29:1-5).[24] While much of this material is redactional, there are reasons for seeing this as a chronistic concern, and the encouragement David offers to Solomon, to complete the task he has so diligently prepared for, serves to strengthen the unity of this period in the complementary reigns of the two kings.

Thus, these speeches serve to demonstrate the smooth transference of power from David to Solomon in marked contrast to the chaotic picture of the so-called "Succession Narrative." It is a time of temple planning for David, and temple building for Solomon, a unity of reigns that mirrors the Chronicler's conception of a United Monarchy comprising both North and South.

Period Two: The Divided Monarchy

Whereas unity characterized Period One, disunity appears as the dominant characterization of Period Two. The limits of this period have already been mentioned as the calls to return presented by Abijah (2 Chr 13:4-12) and Hezekiah (2 Chr 30:6-9). Of crucial importance is the recognition that each of these speeches occurs after a disastrous event that threatened the unity of the kingdom described in Period One. Abijah's speech occurs after the North's willful rebellion after the schism of 922,

---

[23]Cf. Plöger, 56.
[24]Ibid., 57.

as Williamson has shown, and Hezekiah's speech occurs at an equally pregnant moment in Israel's history, the fall of the North in 722.

Several other observations argue for the parenthetic nature of these speeches. In the analysis of Royal Speech it was observed that the Chronicler has a predilection for introductory vocatives, historical retrospects and a hortatory tone in his speeches. All three of these elements occur together only in these two speeches and 2 Chr 29:5-11, Hezekiah's address to the Levites which re-establishes the cult and makes his call for a Northern return possible. Also, when the references to Solomon after the Solomonic Era are tabulated,[25] it is immediately obvious that no comparisons are made to Solomon after Abijah's speech (2 Chr 13:6, 7) or before Hezekiah's speech. In fact, the first comparison to Solomon after the period of Abijah is made with reference to Hezekiah himself as a result of the response of all Israel to Hezekiah's speech:

> So there was great joy in Jerusalem, for since the time of Solomon the son of David king of Israel there had been nothing like this in Jerusalem (2 Chr 30:26).

The key word in this period, if not in Chronicles as a whole, is דרש. Of the 165 or so occurrences of this verbal root in the Old Testament, forty are in Chronicles.[26] In the Old Testament, דרש is usually a technical term for a special enquiry, especially by a prophet.[27] This is the sense in which דרש appears at 1 Chr 10:14; 2 Chr 31:9; 32:31; 34:21, 26. However, the other thirty-five occurrences in Chronicles cannot be reconciled with this technical usage. They seem to employ a more generalized usage that is somehow involved with being faithful, seeking God "in the various exercises and offices of religion,"[28] for example, in 2 Chr 14:3 Asa's reform measures, which are not paralleled in the Kings account, are prefaced by the command to "seek Yahweh" and the contents of the covenant that king struck as a result of the reform are summarized with:

> And they entered into a covenant to seek Yahweh, the God of their fathers, with all their heart and with all their soul; and

---

[25]2 Chr 10:2, 6; 11:3, 17, 17; 12:9; 13:6, 7; 30:26; 33:7; 35:3, 4.

[26]Claus Westermann, "Die Begriffe für Fragen und Suchen im AT," *Kerygma und Dogma* 6 (1960) 2-30, especially 14ff.

[27]Samuel E. Driver, *An Introduction to the Literature of the Old Testament,* 9th ed. rev. (Edinburgh: T & T Clark, 1913) 536.

[28]Ibid.

that whoever would not seek Yahweh, the God of their
fathers, should be put to death, whether young or old, man or
woman (2 Chr 15:12f).

As S. Wagner notices:

That the Chronicler understands "seeking Yahweh" in a broad
sense is also indicated by the fact that in parallel expressions
very different activities help to define its material content.[29]

"Walking in the commandments of God" (2 Chr 17:4), "keeping torah"
(2 Chr 14:3), "destroying Asherahs" (2 Chr 19:3), "keeping Yahweh's word"
(1 Chr 10:13f) and "building the temple and establishing the cult" (1 Chr
28:9) are all related to the concept of דרש.

For the purposes of this chapter, a listing of the chronistic opposites to
דרש as they appear in word pairs is informative. Three terms in particular
are significant. עזב "to forsake" like דרש, has lost some of its specificity
in Chronicles and occurs as a general term summarizing the apostasy of
the king, for example in 2 Chr 21:10; 28:6 where it is stated, "because he
(they) had forsaken Yahweh, the God of their fathers." There are references to specific apostasy in Chronicles, most notably, the failure to keep
torah (2 Chr 12:1, 5) and failure to esteem the Jerusalem temple (2 Chr
13:4-12), Abijah's summons to return where the contrast between the
North's forsaking of the cult and the South's "not forsaking" is dramati-
cally drawn. 2 Chr 24:18, however, depicts Judah as forsaking the house of
Yahweh as does 2 Chr 29:6-7 in Hezekiah's summary of the apostasy of
Ahaz. Thus, apostasy is not limited to the North. That עזב is to be seen as
an opposite of דרש is shown by 1 Chr 28:9 and 2 Chr 15:2, "If you seek him,
he will be found by you, but if you forsake him, he will forsake you."

מעל "be unfaithful," is even more general than עזב in Chronicles. The
reigns of Ahaz (2 Chr 28:19) and Manasseh (2 Chr 33:19) as well as Judah's
final apostasy are summarized as merely being "unfaithful." מעל is also
conceived as an opposite to דרש as seen in 1 Chr 10:13f:

And Saul died for his unfaithfulness; he was unfaithful to

---

[29]S. Wagner, "דָּרַשׁ, darash," in *Theological Dictionary of the Old
Testament,* ed. G. Johannes Botterweck and Helmer Ringgren, trans. John
T. Willis and Geoffrey W. Bromily (Grand Rapids: William B. Eerdmans,
1978) 3:301.

Yahweh in that he did not keep Yahweh's word, and also
consulted a medium, seeking guidance, but did not seek
Yahweh . . .

Further supporting evidence is found at 2 Chr 28:22-23 (reading with the
LXX):[30]

he became yet more unfaithful to Yahweh, and the king said,
"I will seek the gods of Damascus which have defeated me."

Thirdly, עשה הרע "to do evil" is contrasted with דרש in 2 Chr 12:14:

And he did evil, for he did not set his heart to seek Yahweh.

Finally, P. Welten has seen the close association of דרש with צלח "to
prosper."[31] The result of seeking Yahweh is prosperity. In 2 Chr 26:5 with
reference to Uzziah and 2 Chr 31:21 with reference to Hezekiah דרש and
צלח (Hiphil) are bound together in a cause-effect relationship. Furthermore, prosperity is only granted to those kings in Chronicles who have
sought Yahweh/God.[32]

This observation of the Chronicler's particular usage of דרש can now be
utilized to further support the contention that the Chronicler has used the
Royal Speeches to divide his narrative into periods. The five speeches
included between the parenthesis formed by the *Umkehrreden* of Abijah
and Hezekiah will be shown to form a chiastic structure based upon the
key word דרש.

    a. *Umkehrrede:* Abijah (2 Chr 13:4-12)
        b. Prosperity, due to seeking Yahweh: Asa (2 Chr 14:6)
            c. Example of king seeking Yahweh: Jehoshaphat (2 Chr
               19:6-11)
               d. "Trust and prosper": Jehoshaphat (2 Chr 20:20)
            c'. Example of king not seeking Yahweh: Ahaz (2 Chr 28:23)
        b'. No prosperity, due to not seeking Yahweh: Hezekiah (2 Chr
           29:5-11)
    a'. *Umkehrrede:* Hezekiah (2 Chr 30:6-9)

---

[30]See Chapter 2, 31f.

[31]*Geschichte und Geschichtsdarstellung in den Chronikbüchern,*
WMANT 42 (Neukirchen-Vluyn: Neukirchen Verlag, 1973) 18, 44, 50-51.

[32]Solomon 2 Chr 7:11; Asa 14:6; Jehoshaphat 20:20; Uzziah 26:5;
Hezekiah 31:21.

The similarities of the first pair of speeches, Abijah/Hezekiah (a, a')
have already been discussed. In the second pair, Asa/Hezekiah (b, b'), a
dichotomy between דרש and צלח is established. The burden of Asa's speech
is to encourage Judah to fortify their cities since Yahweh has given them
rest as well as the land because they have sought him. In other words,
they have prospered (צלח) due to their seeking (דרש) Yahweh. On the other
hand, Hezekiah's speech is a condemnation of "our fathers" (v 6), here
meaning Ahaz and those who followed his lead, for not seeking Yahweh.
Though דרש does not occur in this context, the antonyms examined above
(מעל, עשה הרע and עזב) all occur in v 6. The consequences of Ahaz not
seeking Yahweh are the military losses and captivity of verses 8f, in other
words, not prospering.

In the third pair of speeches, Jehoshaphat/Ahaz (c, c'), the key word,
דרש, is again played upon with opposing sets of behavior. 2 Chr 19:3,
Jehu's speech to Jehoshaphat, claims Jehoshaphat has "set his heart to
seek (דרש) God." This becomes the *Stichwort*[33] for the entire reign of
Jehoshaphat, which becomes a paradigmatic reign for all good kings. He
institutes reform and establishes judicial organization, thus mirroring the
united reigns of David and Solomon in Period One. Further indications of
the Chronicler's high esteem for Jehoshaphat include his expansion of the
meager information contained in 1 Kgs 15:24; 22:41-49 and the Miciah ben
Imlah pericope of 1 Kgs 22:1-35 to four chapters; placing two speeches
(2 Chr 19:6-11; 20:20) and a prayer (2 Chr 20:6-12) on his lips; and calling
him a son of David (2 Chr 19:3). On the other hand, Ahaz's short speech
becomes a paradigm of the king who refuses to seek Yahweh but seeks
(דרש) the foreign gods of Damascus.[34] That Ahaz, and not Manasseh as in
Kings, is the arch villain for the Chronicler is well known and need not be
substantiated here.

This leaves Jehoshaphat's pithy speech in 2 Chr 20:20 (d) as the crucial
center of the chiasmus:

> Hear me, Judah and inhabitants of Jerusalem! Believe in the
> Lord, your God and you will be established; believe his proph-
> ets and you will succeed.

While this speech clearly recalls Isa 7:9, especially in the pun on אמן, the
major significance of the speech is that it calls Judah to trust in Yahweh's

---

[33]Plöger, 63.
[34]Reading with the LXX, see 40.

prophets that they might succeed, צלח. An examination of the Chronicler's prophetic speech reveals that in these unique prophetic oracles the same message of retributive justice is repeated again and again.[35] What is crucial to the Chronicler's structuring, however, is the observation that *all* of these prophetic utterances occur here, in Period Two, a period which has, as the chiasmus shows, Jehoshaphat, the paradigmatic king of the period, delivering a Royal Speech to that effect at its center point.

Period Two, then, is best seen as a time when the unity displayed in Period One has been dissolved. The call is for North and South to re-unite by seeking Yahweh and hearing his prophets as Jehoshaphat had done.

Period Three: The Re-united Monarchy

The disunity, which marked Period Two as differing in character from the emphasis on unity displayed in Period One, is resolved, for the Chronicler, in Period Three. As F. L. Moriarty succinctly puts it:

> With the fall of Samaria in 721 B.C. and the deportation of North Israel's leading citizens Judah inherited the burden of sustaining alone the ideal of a state under the rule of Yahweh.[36]

Historically, there is no longer a division in the kingdom as in Period Two, the North has fallen to Assyria, and Judah, under Ahaz, has apostasized to the point of closing the temple (2 Chr 28:24). Since Judah is still free of Assyrian domination, she provides the only option for a return to the political/cultic unity enjoyed under David and Solomon in Period One. But for that to occur, drastic reform is necessary. Thus, the stage is set for the Chronicler's re-interpretation of the roles of Hezekiah and Josiah.

There has been a lively debate in recent years as to whether the Chronicler's portrayal of Hezekiah seeks to depict him as a "New David" or as a "New Solomon." The three major interpretations will be presented here, again with the purpose of seeing whether they can be synthesized and augmented by insights gained from the study of the Chronicler's Royal Speech and Prayers.

---

[35]See Appendix, below.

[36]"The Chronicler's Account of Hezekiah's Reform," *CBQ* 27 (1965) 399.

III. HEZEKIAH: NEW DAVID OR NEW SOLOMON?

R. Mosis

The most detailed attempt to see Hezekiah as a second David is that of R. Mosis.[37] This is a corollary to his suggestion that the Chronicler has adopted the reigns of Saul, David and Solomon as paradigms of three possible situations in which Israel might find herself (165). The period of Saul is the period of apostasy, the period of David serves as a model for the good king and that of Solomon is reserved to portray the period of final blessing, a period which later Israel can only hope for in faith. Since this final realization must remain future oriented, the subsequent kings of Judah must, in Mosis's reconstruction, be patterned on either Saul or David. Thus, Mosis calls Hezekiah, "einen zweiten David" (189), on the basis of the following evidence (189-192):

1. 2 Chr 29:2 claims Hezekiah "did that which was right in the eyes of Yahweh, according to all that David his father had done"

2. After claiming the post-exilic restoration of the Jerusalem cult in Ezra 1-6 is "Davidic," Mosis displays the parallels between this restoration and Hezekiah's cleansing of the temple and Passover

3. 2 Chr 32:1-23, the salvation of Hezekiah and Jerusalem from Sennacherib is thought to parallel 1 Chr 14 in that both describe a victory as the result of seeking Yahweh/Ark. If Hezekiah were to parallel Solomon "the man of peace," Mosis thinks the Assyrian invasion would be impossible

H. G. M. Williamson.

The strongest argument against seeing Hezekiah as a second David as well as for seeing him as a second Solomon is that of H. G. M. Williamson.[38] After a review of Mosis's position, Williamson faults Mosis for passing over the contrary evidence which points to the Chronicler's patterning of Hezekiah's reign on that of Solomon.

1. 2 Chr 30:26 states that after Hezekiah's celebration of the Passover, "there was great joy in Jerusalem, for since the time of Solomon the son of David king of Israel there had been nothing like this in Jerusalem"

2. The temple arrangements established by the two kings are identical

---

[37] *Untersuchungen.*
[38] *Israel,* 119-125.

3. 2 Chr 31:2, which deals with Hezekiah's appointment of the priests and Levites, recalls 2 Chr 8:14 in the reign of Solomon[39]

4. 2 Chr 32:27-29 emphasizes the wealth of Hezekiah much as 2 Chr 9:13ff does for Solomon

5. While Williamson makes no judgment on Mosis's estimate of the Chronicler's portrayal of the attitude of the Gentiles to the king of Israel as anticipating the prophetic hope of the pilgrimage of the nations to Jerusalem (155-162), he shows the similarity of 2 Chr 9:23f, which describes all the kings of the earth bringing gifts to Solomon, with 2 Chr 32:23, which describes a similar activity on Hezekiah's behalf

6. The Chronicler regards the time of Hezekiah as one in which the land was restored for the first time to its geographical extent in the time of Solomon

Williamson then dismisses Mosis's arguments, one by one:[40]

1. The remark that Hezekiah did "according to all that David his father had done" is taken from the Chronicler's source (2 Kgs 18:3)

2. Williamson denies the common authorship of Chronicles and Ezra and remarks that, "the Chronicler was fully justified in explicitly drawing the parallels between these events (i.e., the cleansing of the temple and the Passover) and the celebration under Solomon"(125, parenthesis added).

3. As for Hezekiah's involvement in the Assyrian Crisis, Williamson notes that the Chronicler omits Hezekiah's initial capitulation (2 Kgs 18:14-16), implies that no cities were captured (2 Chr 32:1 simply says Sennacherib "encamped against the fortified cities, *thinking* to win them for himself"), and records, with Kings, that victory was due to the intervention of Yahweh, not Hezekiah's military activities. Thus, Hezekiah, too, can be called a "man of peace," especially since the Chronicler records Solomon "went to Hamath-zobah, and prevailed against it" (2 Chr 8:3, no parallel).

P. R. Ackroyd

A mediating position is taken by Ackroyd who sees in the reign of Hezekiah a new David and a new Solomon.[41] In support of his contention

---

[39]The force of this argument is considerably weakened if Willi's assignment of 2 Chr 8:14 and much of 2 Chr 31:2 to a later hand is correct, as I think it is, see Willi, 197.

[40]*Israel*, 124-125.

[41]*Chronicles*, 179-189.

that Hezekiah is a new David, Ackroyd points to 2 Chr 29:1-2 as the first
stage of a reform designed to reverse the policies of Ahaz, and a return to
a situation similar to David's as had Mosis. Secondly, he notices the intention of 2 Chr 29:25-30 is to relate the restoration of the temple music
back to the commands of David, as Mosis had argued (72-73). Williamson's
critique of both these points is persuasive, but Ackroyd adds a third, not
employed by Mosis. In 2 Chr 31:2, Ackroyd discerns the basis of
Hezekiah's reordering of the priests and the Levites to be David's estab-
lishment of these offices in 1 Chr 23-27, not Solomon's appointment in
2 Chr 8:14 as in Williamson's reconstruction. Willi's assignment of the
2 Chr texts to a later hand has been offered as a refutation of
Williamson's position and may be so employed here to refute Ackroyd as
1 Chr 23-27 is surely a later expansion.

In support of his contention that Hezekiah is a second Solomon,
Ackroyd makes use of many of the same arguments Williamson employed
as well as three additional ones:

1. In 2 Chr 29:18, which deals with the recovery of the temple vessels,
Ackroyd states:

> The vessels represent the continuity of the worship of the
> temple with the past, for it was at the building of the temple
> by Solomon that proper provision was made for them.[42]

2. In 2 Chr 30:18-20, Ackroyd sees Hezekiah's intercessory prayer for
those participants who were unclean as reminiscent of Solomon's great
prayer in 2 Chr 6.

3. In 2 Chr 30:27, the priestly blessing in which "the prayer came to his
holy habitation in heaven," echoes the refrain of Solomon's prayer in 2 Chr
6.

On the basis of the preceding analysis it is clear that Mosis's position of
seeing Hezekiah only as a second David cannot be maintained. Furthermore, the additional support offered by Ackroyd, with regard to the
Davidic interpretation, has also been found inconclusive. But is the solution to be found in Williamson's position of seeing Hezekiah as only a
second Solomon? While Williamson's conclusion that the Chronicler has
solved the problem of the Divided Monarchy in his reinterpretation of the
Hezekiah material to yield a restoration of the position lost at the Schism
is persuasive, it is not dependent upon seeing Hezekiah as a second

---

[42]Ibid., 182.

Solomon alone. If the analysis of Period One shows the crucial point to be the unity of David *and* Solomon, we should expect something of the same sort in Period Three, the Re-united Monarchy. That this is the case can be shown from the evidence contained in the Royal Speeches of the period.

Hezekiah: New David and New Solomon

In Hezekiah's speech (2 Chr 32:7-8), v 7, "Be strong and courageous, do not fear or be dismayed . . ." is exactly equivalent to David's words of encouragement to Solomon in 1 Chr 22:13, except that David's imperatives are in the singular while Hezekiah's are in the plural. This alteration in number is due to the respective audiences of each speech. Furthermore, the first pair of imperatives is repeated in 1 Chr 28:20 again, where David is encouraging his son. The second pair of imperatives occurs in the same verse, separated only by "and do," which refers to the building of the temple and is not relevant to Hezekiah's audience. Finally, in v 8, the phrase, "for the Lord our God is with us," is equivalent to 1 Chr 22:18, where David encourages the leaders of Israel, and is similar to 1 Chr 28:20, "for the Lord God (my God) is with you (singular)," where David encourages Solomon. Throughout this section there is an emphasis upon all Israelites, North and South, participating in the political and cultic structure as shown by the covenant making activities of Hezekiah and Josiah, as well as their extensive Passovers.

This speech of Hezekiah's, with its clear references to the speeches of David, provides proof of the Davidic coloring of his reign. When this is taken in conjunction with the many Solomonic references produced by Williamson and Ackroyd, a picture of Hezekiah as both a new David and a new Solomon clearly emerges, and marks Period Three as a re-unification, similar to Period One.

The two speeches of Josiah contained in this period also support this contention. In his first speech (2 Chr 34:21), which the Chronicler has taken over from his source (2 Kgs 22:13), there is a tendentious change: the reference to "those who are left in Israel and in Judah." The addition of the reference to the remnant in Israel (which also occurs at v 9) was introduced to emphasize the unity of North and South that is now present in Period Three. In his second speech (2 Chr 35:3a, 5b-6), Josiah's re-establishment of the priesthood along the lines of David in Period One completes the recollection of the United Monarchy.

IV. SUMMARY

Thus, the Chronicler's periodization of history, as schematized in the Royal Speeches, pictures the monarchy as moving from political unity through disunity and back again to unity in three periods:

1. The United Monarchy, where emphasis on the unity of David and Solomon as characteristic of the unity of North and South is uppermost.

2. The Divided Monarchy, where the only hope for unity lies in "seeking Yahweh" as has Jehoshaphat, the paradigmatic king of the period, in accordance with the word of God through the prophets.

3. The Re-united Monarchy, where Hezekiah and Josiah are pictured as comprising elements of both David and Solomon, and work towards the unified state.

Appendix:
Prophetic Speech in Chronicles

Past attempts to analyze the speeches contained in the books of Chronicles have tended to place indiscriminately all the occurrences of direct discourse together in one category, or at best, to differentiate only between speech and prayer. Thus, in von Rad's essay, speeches made by prophets and prayers are all examined under the rubric of the "Levitival Sermon."[1] Plöger, while formally distinguishing between speeches and prayers, does not distinguish between prophetic speech and Royal speech,[2] and neither of these studies attempts a comprehensive investigation.

However, the majority of speeches spoken by prophets are attributed to messengers completely unknown to us outside the Chronicler's work. This is especially true of the ten speeches that occur within the parenthesis formed by the *Umkehrreden* of 2 Chr 13:4-12 and 30:6-9. Within this section of the "The Divided Monarchy," in contrast to the vibrant prophetic speech of the past,[3] the Chronicler has portrayed these otherwise unknown prophets as all speaking the same message, namely, his doctrine of retributive justice. This similarity is best seen in a schematic arrangement of the texts:

1. Azariah (2 Chr 15:1-7)
   a. v 2: "The Lord is with you, while you are with him. If you seek him, he will be found by you . . ." (positive use)

---

[1]Von Rad, "Levitical Sermon."
[2]Plöger, "Reden und Gebete."
[3]For a form critical examination of the Chronicler's prophetic speech compared to that of classical prophecy, see Braun, "Significance," 232-239.

      b. v 2: ". . . but if you forsake him, he will forsake you." (negative use)

      c. v 7: ". . . for your work shall be rewarded." (positive use)

2.   Hanani (2 Chr 16:7-9)

      a. v 7: Becuase Asa relied upon Ben-Hadad instead of God, he lost to Aram. (negative use)

      b. v 8: When Asa relied upon God against the Ethiopians, he had victory. (positive use)

3.   Jehu (2 Chr 19:2-3)

      a. v 2: Because Jehoshaphat helped the wicked (i.e., Ahab) and loved those that hate Yahweh (i.e., Ahab's followers), wrath will be upon him (i.e., the invasion of chapter 20). (negative use)

      b. v 3: Because Jehoshaphat put away the Asheroth and set his heart to seek God, good things are found in him. (positive use)

4.   Jahaziel (2 Chr 20:14-17)

      a. v 15: Because Jehoshaphat prayed in the temple, the message is a Salvation Oracle, "Fear not . . . the battle is God's . . . see the victory of Yahweh." (positive use)

5.   Eliezer (2 Chr 20:37)

      a. v 37: Because Jehoshaphat aligned himself with Ahaziah, his ships were sunk. (negative use)

6.   Elijah's Epistle (2 Chr 21:12-15)

      a. v 12-15: Because Jeroboam walked in the ways of the kings of Israel, Yahweh will strike the people, children, wives and substance with plague. (negative use)

7.   Zechariah (2 Chr 24:20)

      a. v 20b: "Because you have forsaken the Lord, he has forsaken you." (negative use)

8.   Man of God (2 Chr 25:8)[4]

      a. v 8: "But if you suppose that in this way you will be strong for war, God will cast you down before the enemy . . ." (negative use)

---

[4]The MT which reads, "But if you go, act, be strong for the battle . . ." (v 8a) is somewhat corrupt. The RSV reconstructs the text along the lines of the LXX by replacing "go (בא)" with "in this way" (באלה or בזות or בס) and reading the imperatives "act" and "be strong" as participles with Rudolph, 278.

9. Prophet (2 Chr 25:15f.)
   a. v 16: "God has determined to destroy you, because you have done this [worshipping useless gods from a people he had defeated, v 15] and have not listened to my counsel." (negative use)
10. Oded (2 Chr 28:9-11) addressed to the North
   a. v 9: The reason for Israel's victory over Judah was Judah's apostasy. (negative use)
   b. v 11: If Israel keeps Judah captive, the Israelites' sin will bring punishment. (negative use)

As this schematic shows, the Chronicler's prophetic speeches, in this period of the Divided Monarchy, are all variations on the theme of retributive justice.

Bibliography

I. TEXTS AND REFERENCE WORKS

Biblia Hebraica, edidit Rudolf Kittel, Textum Masoreticum curavit P. Kahle. Editio duodecima emendata typis editionis septimae expressa. Stuttgart: Privilegierte Württembergische Bibelanstalt, 1963.

Brown, Francis; Driver, Samuel R.; and Briggs, Charles A., eds. *A Hebrew Lexicon of the Old Testament.* Based on the Lexicon of William Gesenius, as translated by Edward Robinson. Oxford: The Clarendon Press, 1957.

De Lagarde, Paul. *Librorum Veteris Testamenti Canonicorum pars prior Graece.* Göttingen: Dietrich Arnold Hoyer, 1882.

Hatch, Edwin, and Redpath, Henry A. *A Concordance to the Septuagint and the other Greek Versions of the Old Testament (Including the Apocryphal Books) and Supplement.* Unveränderte Nachdruck der in 1897 in Oxford, Clarendon Press erschienenen Ausgabe. Graz, Austria: Akademische Druck-und Verlagsanstalt, 1954. 2 volumes.

Josephus, Flavius. *The Works of Flavius Josephus.* Translated by William Whiston. Chicago: The John C. Winston Co., n.d.

Kautsch, Emil, ed. *Gesenius' Hebrew Grammar.* 2d English ed. Translated and revised by A. E. Cowley. Oxford: Oxford University Press, 1910.

Le Déaut, Roger, and Robert, J. *Targum des Chroniques, Tome II.* Analecta Biblica no. 51. Rome: Biblical Institute Press, 1971.

Liddel, Henry G., and Scott, Robert. *A Greek-English Lexicon.* 9th Edition. Revised and Augmented throughout by Sir Henry Stuart Jones. Oxford: The Clarendon Press, 1940.

Mandelkern, Solomon. *Veteris Testamenti Concordantiae Hebraicae Atque Chaldaicae.* Post F. Margolinii et M. Gottsteinii Editiones. Editio Sixta Aucta Atque Emendata. Tel-Aviv: Sumptibus Schocken Hierosolymis, 1964.

The Oxford Annotated Bible with the Apocrypha, Revised Standard Version. Edited by Herbert G. May and Bruce M. Metzger. New York: Oxford University Press, 1965.

Vannutelli, Primus. *Libri Synoptici Veteris Testamenti seu Librorum Regum et Chronicorum Loci Paralleli. Quos Hebraice Graece et Latine Critice Edidit.* 2 volumes. Rome: Pontifical Biblical Institute, 1931 and 1934.

Williams, Ronald J. *Hebrew Syntax, An Outline,* 2d ed. Toronto: University of Toronto Press, 1976.

II. COMMENTARIES ON THE BOOKS OF CHRONICLES

Ackroyd, Peter R. *I & II Chronicles, Ezra, Nehemiah: Introduction and Commentary.* Torch Bible Commentaries. London: SCM Press, 1973.

Barnes, William E. *The Books of Chronicles.* The Cambridge Bible for Schools and Colleges. Cambridge: Cambridge University Press, 1899.

Benzinger, Immanuel G. A. *Die Bücher der Chronik.* Kurzer Hand-Commentar zum Alten Testament, Abt 20. Tübingen: J. C. B. Mohr (Paul Siebeck), 1901.

Coggins, Richard J. *The First and Second Books of the Chronicles.* The Cambridge Bible Commentary on the New English Bible. Cambridge: Cambridge University Press, 1976.

Curtis, Edward L., and Madsen, Albert A. *A Critical and Exegetical Commentary on the Books of Chronicles.* International Critical Commentary. New York: Charles Scribner's Sons, 1910.

Galling, Kurt. *Die Bücher der Chronik, Esra, Nehemia.* Das Alte Testament Deutsch, T. 12. Göttingen: Vandenhoeck und Ruprecht, 1954.

Goettsberger, Johann. *Die Bücher der Chronik oder Paralipomenon.* Die Heilige Schrift des Alten Testaments, Bd 4, Abt 1. Bonn: Peter Hanstein Verlagsbuchhandlung, 1939.

Harvey-Jellie, Wallace R. *Chronicles.* The Century Bible. Edinburgh: T. C. & E. C. Jack, 1906.

Keil, Carl F. *The Books of the Chronicles.* Translated by Andrew Harper. Clarks' Foreign Theological Library, Ser. 4, Vol. 7. Edinburgh: T & T Clark, 1872.

Kittel, Rudolph, *Die Bücher der Chronik.* Handkommentar zum Alten Testament, Abt 1, Bd 6, T 1. Göttingen: Vandenhoeck und Ruprecht, 1902.

Michaeli, Frank. *Les Livres des Chroniques, d'Esdras, et de Nehemie.* Commentaire de l'Ancien Testament. Neuchatel: Delachaux & Niestlé, 1967.

Myers, Jacob M. *I Chronicles.* The Anchor Bible, Vol. 12. Garden City: Doubleday, 1965.

_____ *II Chronicles.* The Anchor Bible, Vol. 13. Garden City: Doubleday, 1965.

Rothstein, Johannes Wilhelm und Hänel, Johannes. *Das Erste Buch der Chronik.* Sellins Kommentar zum Alten Testament, Bd 18, T 2. Leipzig: A. Deichert, 1927.

Rudolph, Wilhelm. *Chronikbücher.* Handbuch zum Alten Testament, Erste Reihe, 21. Tübingen: Verlag von J. C. B. Mohr (Paul Siebeck), 1955.

Slotki, I. W. *Chronicles: Hebrew Text & English Translation with an Introduction and Commentary.* Soncino Books of the Bible. London: The Soncino Press, 1952.

III. BOOKS

Ackroyd, Peter R. *Exile and Restoration. A Study of Hebrew Thought of the Sixth Century B.C.* Old Testament Library. Philadelphia: Westminster Press, 1968.

Allen, Leslie C. *The Greek Chronicles: The Relation of the Septuagint of I and II Chronicles to the Massoretic Text. Part I: The Translator's Craft.* Supplements to Vetus Testamentum, Vol. 25. Leiden, E. J. Brill, 1974.

_____ *The Greek Chronicles: The Relation of the Septuagint of I and II Chronicles to the Massoretic Text. Part II: Textual Criticism.* Supplements to Vetus Testamentum, Vol. 27. Leiden, E. J. Brill, 1974.

Beuken, W. A. M. *Haggai-Sacharja 1-8: Studien zur Überlieferungsgeschichte der frünachexilischen Prophetie.* Studia Semitica Neerlandica 10. Assen: Van Gorcum, 1967.

Bright, John. *A History of Israel.* 2d ed. Philadelphia: The Westminster Press, 1972.

Carlson, R. A. *David, the Chosen King. A Traditio-Historical Approach to the Second Book of Samuel.* Translated by Eric J. Sharpe and Stanley Rudman. Stockholm: Almqvist & Wiksell, 1964.

Childs, Brevard S. *Introduction to the Old Testament as Scripture.* Philadelphia: Fortress Press, 1979.

Cross, Frank M., Jr. *Canaanite Myth and Hebrew Epic: Essays in the History of the Religion of Israel*. Cambridge: Harvard University Press, 1973.

Cross, Frank M., Jr., and Talmon, Shemaryahu, eds. *Qumran and the History of the Biblical Text*. Cambridge: Harvard University Press, 1975.

Döller, Johannes. *Das Gebet im Alten Testament*. Theologische Studien der Osterreichischen Leo-Gesellschaft, hrsg. von Martin Grabmann und Theodor Innitzer, Bd 21. Hildesheim: Verlag Dr. H. A. Gerstenberg. n.d.

Driver, Samuel R. *An Introduction to the Literature of the Old Testament*. 9th ed. rev. Edinburgh: T & T Clark, 1913.

Ehrlich, Arnold B. *Randglossen zur hebraischen Bibel, textkritisches, sprachliches und sachliches*. Bd 7. Leipzig: J. C. Hinrich, 1914.

Eissfeldt, Otto. *The Old Testament. An Introduction*. Translated by Peter R. Ackroyd from the 3rd edition (1964) of *Einleitung in das Alte Testament*, first published in 1934. New York: Harper & Row, 1965.

Encyclopedia Judiaca. S.v. "Chronicles, Book of," by Sara Japhet.

Gray, John. *I & II Kings*. 2d ed. Old Testament Library. Philadelphia: The Westminster Press, 1971.

_____ *The Legacy of Canaan*. Supplements to Vetus Testamentum, Vol. 5. Leiden: E. J. Brill, 1957.

Johnson, Marshall D. *The Purpose of the Biblical Genealogies*. Society for New Testament Study Monograph Series, no. 8. Cambridge: Cambridge University Press, 1969.

Kidner, Derek. *Ezra and Nehemiah: An Introduction and Commentary*. Tyndale Old Testament Library. Downers Grove: InterVarsity Press, 1979.

Krinetzki, Leo. *Israels Gebet im Alten Testament*. Aschaffenburg: Paul Pattloch Verlag, 1965.

Kropat, Arno. *Die Syntax des Autors der Chronik vergleichen mit seiner Quellen*. Zeitschrift für die alttestamentliche Wissenschaft, Beiheft 16. Giessen: Alfred Töpelmann, 1909.

Mosis, Rudolph. *Untersuchungen zur Theologie des chronistischen Geschichtswerkes*. Freiburger theologisches Studien, Bd 92. Freiburg: Herder, 1972.

Noth, Martin. *Überlieferungsgeschichtliche Studien I. Die sammelnden und bearbeitenden Geschichtswerke im Alten Testament.* Halle: Max Niemeyer Verlag, 1943.

Olmstead, Albert T. *History of the Persian Empire.* Chicago: University of Chicago Press, 1948.

Petersen, David L. *Late Israelite Prophecy: Studies in Deutero-Prophetic Literature and in Chronicles.* Society of Biblical Literature Monograph Series, no. 23. Missoula: Scholars, 1977.

Pohlmann, Karl-Friedrich. *Studien zum dritten Esra. Ein Beitrag zur Frage nach dem ursprunglichen Schluss des chronistischen Geschichtswerkes.* Forschungen zur Religion und Literatur des Alten und Neuen Testaments, Bd 104. Göttingen: Vandenhoeck & Ruprecht, 1970.

Polzin, Robert. *Late Biblical Hebrew: Toward an Historical Typology of Biblical Hebrew Prose.* Harvard Semitic Monographs, no. 12. Missoula: Scholars, 1976.

Rad, Gerhard von. *Das Geschichtsbild des chronistischen Werkes.* Beiträge zur Wissenschaft von Alten und Neuen Testament, Bd 54. Stuttgart: W. Kohlhammer, 1930.

Rehm, Martin. *Textkritische Untersuchungen zu den Parallelstellen der Samuel-Konigsbucher und der Chronik.* Altestestamentliche Abhandlungen, Bd 13, Abt 3. Münster: Aschendorff, 1937.

Ulrich, Eugene C. *The Qumran Text of Samuel and Josephus.* Harvard Semitic Monographs, no. 19. Missoula: Scholars, 1978.

Welch, Adam C. *Post-Exilic Judaism.* The Baird Lecture, 1934. Edinburgh: William Blackwood and Sons, 1935.

_____ *The Work of the Chronicler. Its Purpose and its Date.* The Schweich Lectures, 1938. London: Oxford University Press, 1939.

Wellhausen, Julius. *Prolegomena to the History of Ancient Israel.* Translated by Black and Menzies from a revised edition of *Geschichte Israels, I,* first published in 1878. Cleveland: Meridian Books, 1957.

Welten, Peter. *Geschichte und Geschichtsdarstellung in der Chronikbuchern.* Wissenschaftliche Monographien zum Alten und Neuen Testament, Bd 42. Neukirchen-Vluyn: Neukirchen Verlag, 1973.

Willi, Thomas. *Die Chronik als Auslegung: Untersuchungen zur literarischen Gestaltung der historischen Uberlieferung Israels.* Forschungen zur Religion und Literatur des Alten und Neuen Testaments, Bd 106. Göttingen: Vandenhoeck & Ruprecht, 1972.

Williamson, H. G. M. *Israel in the Books of Chronicles*. Cambridge: Cambridge University Press, 1977.

Wilson, Robert R. *Genealogy and History in the Biblical World*. Yale Near Eastern Researches, no. 7. New Haven: Yale University Press, 1977.

Wyk, Wouter C. van, ed. *Studies in the Chronicler*. Ou-Testamentiese Werkgemeenskap in Suider-Afrika, Bd 19, Old Testament Essays. Hercules: Weeshuispers.

Zunz, Leopold. "Dibre hajamim oder die Bücher der Chronik." First published in 1832. In *Die gottesdienstlichen Vorträge der Juden, historisch entwickelt. Ein Beitrag zur Altertumskunde und biblischen Kritik, zur Literatur-und Religionsgeschichte*, pp. 13-36. Zweite, nach dem Handexemplar des Verfassers berichtige und mit einem Register vermehrte Auflage. Hrsg. von N. Brull. Frankfort a. M.: Verlag von J. Kauffmann, 1892.

IV. ARTICLES AND ESSAYS

Ackroyd, Peter R. "The Chronicler as Exegete." *Journal for the Study of the Old Testament* 2 (1977) 2-32.

_____ "History and Theology in the Writings of the Chronicler." *Concordia Theological Monthly* 38 (1967) 501-515.

_____ "The Temple Vessels - a continuity theme." In *Studies in the Religion of Ancient Israel*, pp. 166-181. Supplements to Vetus Testamentum, Vol. 23. Leiden: E. J. Brill, 1972.

_____ "The Theology of the Chronicler." *Lexington Theological Quarterly* 8 (1973) 101-116.

_____ "Two Old Testament Historical Problems of the Early Persian Period." *Journal of Near Eastern Studies* 17 (1958) 13-27.

Albright, William F. "The Date and the Personality of the Chronicler." *Journal of Biblical Literature* 40 (1921) 104-124.

_____ "The Judicial Reform of Jehoshaphat (2 Chron. 19:5-11)." In *Alexander Marx Jubilee Volume*, English Section, 61-82. Edited by Saul Lieberman. New York: Jewish Theological Seminary of America Press, 1950.

Begrich, Joachim. "Das priesterliche Heilsorakel." *Zeitschrift für die alttestamentliche Wissenschaft*, Bd 52 (1934) 81-92.

Braun, Roddy L. "Chronicles, Ezra, and Nehemiah: Theology and Literary History." In *Studies in the Historical Books of the Old Testament*, pp. 52-64. Supplements to Vetus Testamentum, Vol. 30. Edited by John A. Emerton. Leiden: E. J. Brill, 1979.

_____ "The Message of Chronicles: Rally 'Round the Temple." *Concordia Theological Monthly* 42 (1971) 502-513.

_____ "A Reconstruction of the Chronicler's Attitude towards the North." *Journal of Biblical Literature* 96 (1977) 59-62.

_____ "Solomon, the Chosen Temple Builder: The Significance of I Chronicles 22, 28, and 29 for the Theology of Chronicles." *Journal of Biblical Literature* 95 (1976) 581-590.

_____ "Solomonic Apologetic in Chronicles." *Journal of Biblical Literature* 92 (1973) 503-516.

Brunet, Adrien M. "Le Chroniste et ses sources." *Revue Biblique* 60 (1953) 481-508; 61 (1954) 349-386.

_____ "La theologie du Chroniste. Theocratie et messianisme." *Sacra Pagina* 1 (1959) 384-397.

Büchler, Adolf. "Zur Geschichte der Tempelmusik und der Tempelpsalmen." *Zeitschrift für die alttestamentliche Wissenschaft* 19 (1899) 96-133, 329-344; 20 (1900) 97-135.

Cross, Frank M., Jr. "A Reconstruction of the Judean Restoration." *Journal of Biblical Literature* 94 (1975) 4-18; also published in *Interpretation* 29 (1975) 187-201.

Cross, Frank M., and Wright, George E. "The Boundary and Province Lists of the Kingdom of Judah." *Journal of Biblical Literature* 75 (1956) 202-226.

Dibelius, Martin. "The Speeches in Acts and Ancient Historiography." First published in 1949 (1944). In *Studies in the Acts of the Apostles*, 138-185. Edited by Heinrich Greeven, translated by Mary Ling. London: SCM Press, 1956.

Driver, Samuel R. "The Speeches in Chronicles." *The Expositor*, Fifth Series I (1895) 241-256; II (1896) 286-308.

Freedman, David N. "The Chronicler's Purpose." *Catholic Biblical Quarterly* 23 (1961) 436-442.

Gese, Hartmut. "Zur Geschichte der Kultsänger am zweiten Tempel." In *Abraham unser Vater. Juden und Christen im Gesprach uber die Bibel. Festschrift für Otto Michel zum 60. Geburtstag*, 222-234. Hrsg. von Otto Betz u. a. Leiden: E. J. Brill, 1963.

Goldingay, John. "The Chronicler as a Theologian." *Biblical Theology Bulletin* 5 (1975) 99-126.

Japhet, Sara. "Conquest and Settlement in Chronicles." *Journal of Biblical Literature* 98 (1979) 205-218.

_____ "The Supposed Common Authorship of Chronicles and Ezra-Nehemia Investigated Anew." *Vetus Testamentum* 18 (1968) 330-371.

Lemke, Werner E. "The Synoptic Problem in the Chronicler's History." *Harvard Theological Review* 58 (1965) 349-363.

Moriarty, Fredrick L. "The Chronicler's Account of Hezekiah's Reform." *Catholic Biblical Quarterly* 27 (1965) 199-406.

Myers, Jacob M. "The Kerygma of the Chronicler: History and Theology in the Service of Religion." *Interpretation* 20 (1966) 259-273.

Newsome, James D., Jr. "Toward a New Understanding of the Chronicler and his Purposes." *Journal of Biblical Literature* 94 (1975) 201-217.

North, Robert. "Theology of the Chronicler." *Journal of Biblical Literature* 82 (1963) 369-381.

Noordtzij, Arie. "Les Intentions du Chroniste." *Revue Biblique* 49 (1940) 161-168.

Plöger, Otto. "Reder und Gebete im deuteronomistischen und chronistischen Geschichtswerk." In *Festschrift für Gunther Dehn*, 35-49. Hrsg. von Wilhelm Schneemelcher. Neukirchen: Kreis Moers, 1957; also published in *Aus der Spätzeit des Alten Testaments*, 50-66. Göttingen: Vandenhoeck & Ruprecht, 1975.

Porter, J. R. "Old Testament Historiography." In *Tradition and Interpretation: Essays by Members of the Society for Old Testament Study*, 152-162. Edited by G. W. Anderson. Oxford: Clarendon Press, 1979.

Rad, Gerhard von. "The Levitical Sermon in I and II Chronicles." First published in 1934. In *The Problem of the Hexateuch and Other Essays*, by Gerhard von Rad, 167-180. Translated by E. W. Trueman Dicken. Edinburgh: Oliver and Boyd, 1966.

_____ "There Remains Still a Rest for the People of God: An Investigation of a Biblical Conception." First published in 1933. In *The Problem of the Hexateuch and Other Essays*, by Gerhard von Rad, 94-102. Translated by E. W. Trueman Dicken. Edinburgh: Oliver and Boyd, 1966.

Rudolph, Wilhelm. "Problems of the Books of Chronicles." *Vetus Testamentum* 4 (1954) 401-409.

_____ "Zur Theologie des Chronisten." *Theologische Literaturzeitung* 79 (1954) 285-286.

Sinclair, Lawrence A. "Redaction of Zechariah 1-8." *Biblical Research* 20 (1975) 36-47.

Stinespring, William F. "Eschatology in Chronicles." *Journal of Biblical Literature* 80 (1961) 209-219.

Throntveit, Mark A. "Linguistic Analysis and the Question of Authorship in Chronicles, Ezra and Nehemiah." *Vetus Testamentum* 32 (1982) 201-216.

Torrey, Charles C. "The Chronicler as Editor and as Independent Narrator." *American Journal of Semitic Languages and Literature* 25 (1908-1909) 157-173 and 188-217.

Towner, W. Sibley. "'Blessed BE YHWH' and 'Blessed Art Thou, YHWH': The Modulation of a Biblical Formula." *Catholic Biblical Quarterly* 30 (1968) 386-399.

Wagner, S. " darash." In *Theological Dictionary of the Old Testament*, 3:293-307. Edited by Johannes Botterweck and Helmer Ringgren. Translated by John T. Willis and Geoffrey W. Bromily. Grand Rapids: William B. Eerdmans Publishing Company, 1978.

Welten, Peter. "Lade-Tempel-Jerusalem: Zur Theologie der Chronik-bucher." In *Textgemäss. Aufsätze und Beiträge zur Hermeneutik des Alten Testaments, Festschrift für Ernst Würthwein zum 70 Geburtstag*, 169-183. Hrsg. von A. H. J. Gunneweg und Otto Kaiser. Göttingen: Vandenhoeck und Ruprecht, 1979.

Westermann, Claus. "Die Begriffe fur Fragen und Suchen im AT." *Kerygma und Dogma* 6 (1960) 2-30.

Williamson, H. G. M. "The Accession of Solomon in the Books of Chronicles." *Vetus Testamentum* 26 (1976) 351-361.

_____ "Eschatology in Chronicles." *Tyndale Bulletin* 28 (1977) 115-154.

_____ "A Note on I Chronicles VII 12." *Vetus Testamentum* 23 (1973) 375-379.

_____ "The Origins of the Twenty-four Priestly Courses, A Study of 1 Chronicles xxii-xxvii." In *Studies in the Historical Books of the Old Testament*, 251-268. Supplements to Vetus Testamentum, Vol. 30. Edited by John A. Emerton. Leiden: E. J. Brill, 1979.

_____ "Sources and Redaction in the Chronicler's Genealogy of Judah." *Journal of Biblical Literature* 98 (1979) 351-359.

V. DISSERTATIONS

Braun, Roddy L. "The Significance of I Chronicles 22, 28, and 29 for the Structure and Theology of the Work of the Chronicler." Th.D. dissertation, Concordia Seminary, 1971.

Engler, Hans. "The Attitude of the Chronicler Toward the Davidic Monarchy." Th.D. dissertation, Union Theological Seminary in Virginia, 1967.

Lemke, Werner E. "Synoptic Studies in the Chronicler's History." Th.D. dissertation, Harvard Univeristy, 1963.

Newsome, James D., Jr. "The Chronicler's View of Prophecy." Ph.D. dissertation, Vanderbilt University, 1973.

Rigsby, Richard O. "The Historiography of Speeches and Prayers in the Books of Chronicles." Th.D. dissertation, Southern Baptist Theological Seminary, 1973.

Scripture Index